Target
Get back on track

GRADE 9

AQA GCSE (9–1)
Spanish

Reading

Viv Halksworth

D1477296

20 17003 614

NEW COLLEGE, SWINDON

Pearson

Published by Pearson Education Limited, 80 Strand, London, WC2R 0RL.

www.pearsonschoolsandfecolleges.co.uk

Text and illustrations © Pearson Education Ltd 2018
Typeset by Newgen KnowledgeWorks Pvt. Ltd., Chennai, India
Produced by Out of House Publishing

The right of Viv Halksworth to be identified as author of this work has been asserted by her in accordance with the
Copyright, Designs and Patents Act 1988.

First published 2018

21 20 19 18
10 9 8 7 6 5 4 3 2 1

British Library Cataloguing in Publication Data
A catalogue record for this book is available from the British Library

ISBN 978 1292 24603 1

Copyright notice
All rights reserved. No part of this publication may be reproduced in any form or by any means (including photocopying
or storing it in any medium by electronic means and whether or not transiently or incidentally to some other use of
this publication) without the written permission of the copyright owner, except in accordance with the provisions of the
Copyright, Designs and Patents Act 1988 or under the terms of a licence issued by the Copyright Licensing Agency,
Barnard's Inn, 86 Fetter Lane, London EC4A 1EN (www.cla.co.uk). Applications for the copyright owner's written permission
should be addressed to the publisher.

Printed in Slovakia by Neografia

Acknowledgements
The author and publisher would like to thank the following individuals and organisations for their kind permission to reproduce
copyright material:

Pearson acknowledges use of the following extracts: pages 54 and 70: Alcolea, Ana, Donde aprenden a volar las
gaviotas; © 2007, Anaya Colección Espacio Abierto; **page 55:** Ruiz Zafón, Carlos, La sombra del viento; © 2010, Editorial
Planeta, S.A.; **page 56:** Belli, Gioconda, La mujer habitada; https://www.mujerfariana.org/images/pdf/Gioconda-Belli---La-mujer-
habitada.pdf Accessed [05 April 2018]

Note from the publisher
Pearson has robust editorial processes, including answer and fact checks, to ensure the accuracy of the content in this
publication, and every effort is made to ensure this publication is free of errors. We are, however, only human, and occasionally
errors do occur. Pearson is not liable for any misunderstandings that arise as a result of errors in this publication, but it is our
priority to ensure that the content is accurate. If you spot an error, please do contact us at resourcescorrections@pearson.
com so we can make sure it is corrected.

This workbook has been developed using the Pearson Progression Map and Scale for Spanish.

To find out more about the Progression Scale for Spanish and to see how it relates to indicative
GCSE 9–1 grades go to www.pearsonschools.co.uk/ProgressionServices

Helping you to formulate grade predictions, apply interventions and track progress.

Any reference to indicative grades in the Pearson Target Workbooks and Pearson Progression Services is not to be
used as an accurate indicator of how a student will be awarded a grade for their GCSE exams.

You have told us that mapping the Steps from the Pearson Progression Maps to indicative grades will make it
simpler for you to accumulate the evidence to formulate your own grade predictions, apply any interventions and track
student progress. We're really excited about this work and its potential for helping teachers and students. It is, however,
important to understand that this mapping is for guidance only to support teachers' own predictions of progress and is
not an accurate predictor of grades.

Our Pearson Progression Scale is criterion referenced. If a student can perform a task or demonstrate a skill, we say they
are working at a certain Step according to the criteria. Teachers can mark assessments and issue results with reference
to these criteria which do not depend on the wider cohort in any given year. For GCSE exams however, all Awarding
Organisations set the grade boundaries with reference to the strength of the cohort in any given year. For more information
about how this works please visit: https://www.gov.uk/government/news/setting-standards-for-new-gcses-in-2017

Contents

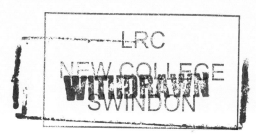

2017003614

LRC
NEW COLLEGE
WITHDRAWN
SWINDON

① Understanding a broad range of vocabulary

This unit will help you to use your knowledge of synonyms, develop your vocabulary and make use of context to work out meaning. The skills you will build are to:

- recognise and understand synonyms
- broaden your vocabulary
- use context to help you identify words you don't know.

In the exam, you will be asked to tackle reading tasks similar to the one on the opposite page. This unit will prepare you to answer matching, selecting and multiple-choice questions, where a broad range of vocabulary is required.

① Comprehension questions often test your skill to link the same ideas expressed using different words. The table below contains phrases from the text in the exam-style question on the opposite page. Match them up with their synonyms in the word box and write ✐ the equivalent phrase in the 'Correct synonym' column.

| casco antiguo   de la mañana a la noche   está a cinco minutos de   invernal   localidad |
| los destinos más turísticos   situado en   tiene   un refugio tranquilo   vista |

Phrase from text	Correct synonym
localizado en	
de invierno	
cuenta con	
panorama	
situación	
centro histórico	
está muy cerca de	
un sitio relajado	
todo el día	
las zonas más visitadas	

Now see how identifying synonyms can help you find the correct answer in a text. Read the exam-style question on page 3 and complete activities ② and ③.

② Look at questions **1–5** following texts **A–G**. For each question:

ⓐ underline Ⓐ the two requirements that each holidaymaker is looking for

ⓑ note down ✐ these requirements in English on paper.

    1 _Luxury accommodation, top quality food_

③ Now read texts **A–G** and underline Ⓐ the aspects described that match the requirements of the holidaymakers.

Do not complete the exam-style question yet. You will be asked to at the end of the unit.

Exam-style question

Ofertas para el verano

Ves estos anuncios en un sitio web español.

A	Situado en la Sierra Nevada, el Hotel Siroco cuenta con los panoramas más exquisitos y los monitores te ayudarán con cualquier deporte invernal que te interese probar.
B	Localidad ideal en pleno casco antiguo, el Hostal Carmen está a cinco minutos de todos los sitios de interés de esta ciudad histórica.
C	Apartamentos María ofrecen un refugio tranquilo, lejos del ruido urbano, donde puedes leer en el balcón viendo ponerse el sol.
D	El Gran Hotel Santiago ofrece un nivel de calidad sin precedentes. Cocina de cinco estrellas cada día, peluquería en la planta baja y gimnasio de uso gratuito.
E	Casa El Palomar te ofrece todas las delicias del campo: productos regionales como el queso y el jamón, actividades relajantes como la equitación y la pesca.
F	Si buscas sol y playa pero prefieres evitar las grandes multitudes de los destinos más turísticos, escoge el Hostal Nerina – un secreto bien guardado.
G	Para que los padres podáis relajaros como merecéis, el Hotel Gaviota cuenta con actividades para los pequeños desde la mañana a la noche. ¡Aprovechadlo!

Escribe la letra correcta en cada casilla.

1 Busco <u>alojamiento de lujo</u> con <u>comida de primera categoría</u>. ⬚ (1 mark)

2 Quiero unos días en un paisaje verde, disfrutando unos pasatiempos rurales. ⬚ (1 mark)

3 Necesitamos descansar y que alguien más cuide a los niños un rato. ⬚ (1 mark)

4 Me gustaría una semana en la costa pero sin miles de veraneantes. ⬚ (1 mark)

5 Siempre me ha interesado el alpinismo y quiero aprender con un instructor. ⬚ (1 mark)

The three key questions in the **skills boosts** will help you recognise and understand a broad range of vocabulary when answering these types of questions.

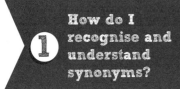
1 How do I recognise and understand synonyms?

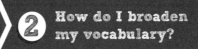
2 How do I broaden my vocabulary?

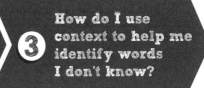
3 How do I use context to help me identify words I don't know?

1 How do I recognise and understand synonyms?

Some more challenging questions require you to match words and phrases that are different but express the same idea. Learning how to identify and understand synonyms will help you.

1 Look at the words in the boxes below.

a Decide whether each word is an adjective, verb or noun, and write 🖉 **A**, **V** or **N** in the box next to each word. Synonyms are usually the same type of word.

b For any words you don't know, note down 🖉 on paper whether they are cognates, or look similar to other Spanish words that you do know.

c Complete 🖉 the table: sort the words into columns so that they are grouped with other words of the same or similar meaning. There should be three words in each column.

piso		estupendo		tormenta		bello		apartamento	N	escoger	
opinar		guapo	A	seleccionar	V	genial		elegir		hermoso	
lluvia	N	hogar		creer		pensar	V	nieve		fenomenal	A

Good looking	To think	Place to live	Weather	Great	To choose
guapo	pensar	apartamento	lluvia	fenomenal	seleccionar

2 Now read the text below, looking carefully at each underlined word or phrase.

> Cada agosto voy con mi familia a <u>veranear</u> ⬚ en la costa. Nos gusta estar <u>a orillas del</u> ⬚
>
> mar y reservamos <u>alojamiento</u> ⬚ <u>junto a</u> ⬚ la playa. Por lo general, pasamos las mañanas
>
> <u>bañándonos</u> ⬚ en el mediterráneo.
>
> Durante las horas de más calor, <u>nos retiramos</u> ⬚ <u>a la sombra</u> ⬚ para <u>almorzar</u> ⬚ unos
>
> platos típicos de <u>gazpacho</u> ⬚ o mariscos.

a Next to each underlined word, write 🖉 **N** for a noun, **A** for an adjective, **AP** for an adverbial phrase and **V** for a verb.

b On paper, write down 🖉 key words from the sentence containing the underlined word. This will help you understand the context. For example:

cada agosto – every August; costa – coast; could refer to a summer holiday.

c Now look at the box below, which contains synonyms for the underlined words/phrases in the text. Annotate 🖉 the text with the synonyms.

nadando	sopa fría	al lado del
habitaciones	cerca de	fuera del sol
nos sentamos	comer	pasar el verano

Use the context and the form of the word to help you replace unfamiliar words with a synonym.

② How do I broaden my vocabulary?

To answer the higher level questions in the exam, you must be familiar with the words that are on the Higher Tier vocabulary list. For example, everyone will know the word *piscina* (swimming pool), but how many students will know the word *sombrilla* (sunshade)?

① The short texts **A–D** below contain some challenging vocabulary from the Higher Tier vocabulary list. In the word box, find the English equivalent for each underlined Spanish word. Write the English meaning in the space provided.

> broken down   to complain   crossroads   customs   disappointed   fan   lorry
> to get a tan   Spanish   to stop   sunshade   sunstroke   wheel   wishes

A El camión [____] estaba averiado [____] en el cruce.
[____] Parecía tener un problema con la rueda [____].

B Como consecuencia de intentar broncearme [____], cogí una insolación [____].
[____] Debería haber usado una sombrilla [____].

C Estuve decepcionado [____] con la manera en que me trataron en la aduana [____].
[____] Voy a quejarme [____] porque no tenían motivo de detenerme [____].

D Buscaba un abanico [____] típico para mi madre pero no podía comunicar
mis deseos [____] ya que en esta región no se habla mucho castellano [____].
[____]

Here are some ideas to help you learn vocabulary:
- Cover up the English and see if you can remember the meaning.
- Cover up the Spanish and see if you can say it out loud.
- Cover up the Spanish and see if you can write the meaning down.
- Get a friend to test you.
- Make flash cards – English on one side, Spanish on the other.
- Record yourself saying the English words, leaving a gap after each word for you to say the Spanish when you play it back.

② Now you are familiar with the Spanish vocabulary, try this: which of the summaries below corresponds to the texts **A–D** in question ①. Write the corresponding letter in the box.

a There was a language barrier problem. [___]

b There was an issue on the road. [___]

c The border officials were in the wrong. [___]

d I had a bit too much sun. [___]

3 **How do I use context to help me identify words I don't know?**

When we come across a word we do not know, we use the information all around it to help us understand what it means. You can use this skill when you come across unfamiliar Spanish words.

① Read sentences **a**–**e** below; each one contains one underlined word. Then:

　i　write down 🖉 whether the underlined word is a noun (**N**), adjective (**A**) or verb (**V**), using the box next to each word. This will help you work out what type of word it is.

　ii　highlight 🖉 all the words/phrases you do know and note 🖉 the translations beneath the sentence.

This will help you understand the general meaning of the sentence.

　a　Mis padres quieren hacer un <u>crucero</u> ⬚ pero odio la idea de pasar una semana en un barco.

....

　b　Vamos a dejar las maletas en la <u>consigna</u> ⬚ mientras comemos en el bar.

....

　c　Quisiera un <u>folleto</u> ⬚ con información turística sobre la ciudad, por favor.

....

　d　Mi padre condujo siempre porque mi madre no tenía su <u>permiso</u> ⬚ .

....

　e　Cuando sales de la estación, tienes que <u>torcer</u> ⬚ a la derecha y cruzar la calle.

....

② You now know the gist of the sentences in ① and the types of word you're looking for.

　a　For the first three sentences, three possible translations for the underlined word are given below. Circle Ⓐ the most likely option.

crucero:	trip	cruise	booking
consigna:	ticket office	platform	left-luggage office
folleto:	leaflet	souvenir	excursion

　b　For the last two sentences, work out the meaning of the underlined words yourself using the skills you've learned. Write 🖉 them below.

　　permiso: ....　　torcer: ....

③ Now write 🖉 a full translation of each sentence in ① on paper and check that they make sense.

Your turn!

Here is an exam-style question that requires you to practise the skills you have worked on, specifically recognising different ways to express the same ideas. ✎

Exam-style question

España como destino turístico

Lees este artículo en una página web española que explica la popularidad de España con los turistas.

Párrafo A	España es un destino turístico desde hace muchos años y, como tal, tiene una buena infraestructura para el turismo con los hoteles, apartamentos, carreteras y centros de ocio para los veraneantes desde campos de golf hasta parques acuáticos. Podemos estar orgullosos de que siempre hay algo que hacer para visitantes de todas las edades.
Párrafo B	No todos los visitantes buscan vacaciones de sol y playa y España tiene un patrimonio variado y rico con sus iglesias, monasterios, catedrales, mezquitas, museos y galerías. Además, ofrece una amplia gama de costumbres y tradiciones muy populares con los visitantes como las fiestas, la gastronomía y la artesanía.
Párrafo C	Lejos de las ciudades y de la costa, España ofrece montañas y valles, praderas y bosques, ríos y tierras áridas. Es un país ideal para el senderismo, la equitación, la pintura y la ornitología. También, el agroturismo (turismo rural) es cada vez más popular.

¿En qué párrafo se expresan las ideas siguientes?

Escribe la letra correcta en cada casilla.

1   No hay que olvidar la cultura histórica y artística del país.   ☐   (1 mark)

2   Lo bueno del país es que todo el mundo puede encontrar algo que le guste.   ☐   (1 mark)

3   España tiene todas las instalaciones necesarias para acoger a sus visitantes.   ☐   (1 mark)

4   La variedad de paisajes y actividades es una atracción creciente.   ☐   (1 mark)

Remember to focus on the key words or phrases in each question and find the section of text that expresses the same idea but in different words. For instance, at the start of paragraph A there is a list of the things that Spain can offer the tourist. This is a list of the **facilities** (*instalaciones*) offered.

There is a wealth of interesting vocabulary on tourism in these passages. To broaden your vocabulary, add any new words to your 'tourism' topic list – try and find synonyms for these as well.

Your turn!

Here is an exam style question that requires you to put in practice the skills you have worked on, specifically recognising Higher Tier vocabulary and using the context to help you understand unfamiliar words.

Exam-style question

An exciting day out

Your Spanish friend, Pascual, shows you the details of an excursion he is going on while on holiday in the USA.

Subiréis lejos de la ciudad en el ferrocarril viejo que, hace un siglo, transportaba a los mineros que excavaban el oro. No os preocupéis por la edad del tren; nunca se ha averiado ni una sola vez. No olvidéis del pasaporte porque durante el viaje cruzaremos la frontera a Canadá y los oficiales de la aduana suben al tren para comprobar los documentos. Una vez llegados al lago, no estaréis decepcionados. Para los más aventureros, hay la oportunidad de hacer piragüismo en el lago y también se ofrecen paseos con un guía que explicará los pájaros y naturaleza que se verán. Para los que simplemente buscan una tarde de descanso, podréis relajaros en el café o tumbaros bajo las sombrillas en la hierba al lado del agua. ¡Un día memorable para todos!

To work out *excavaban*, look at the vocabulary in options A to C in question 1 to help you deduce the context.

Write the correct letter in each box.

1   What was the railway originally used for?

A	carrying gold miners
B	the transport of mining equipment
C	bringing gold down to the city

(1 mark)

2   What evidence is there that the old train still functions well?

A	It hasn't been late once.
B	The engine has been modernised.
C	It has never broken down.

(1 mark)

3   What will happen when you reach the Canadian border?

A	Customs officers will board the train.
B	You will get off to show your passport.
C	You will sign an official border document.

(1 mark)

4   What is on offer for adventure-seeking travellers?

A	hiking with a guide
B	a water sport
C	exploring caves

(1 mark)

5   What is suggested for the less active travellers?

A	bathing in the refreshing waters of the lake
B	trying the local specialities in the café
C	lying in the grass under a sunshade

(1 mark)

Review your skills

Check up

Review your responses to the exam-style questions on pages 7 and 8. Tick ✓ the column that shows how well you think you have done each of the following.

	Not quite ✓	Nearly there ✓	Got it! ✓
recognised and understood synonyms	☐	☐	☐
broadened my vocabulary	☐	☐	☐
used context to help me identify words I didn't know	☐	☐	☐

Need more practice?

Go back to page 3 and complete ✐ the exam-style question there. Use the checklist to help you. ✓

Checklist Before I answer the questions, have I...	✓
paid close attention to words and phrases that express the same ideas in different ways?	
recognised and understood a broad range of vocabulary, including less common words?	
used the context to help me understand words I didn't know?	

To build up your vocabulary, you can create 'word family' cards. For example, this one contains words and phrases relating to transport:

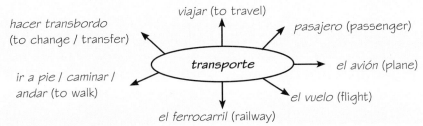

hacer transbordo (to change / transfer)

viajar (to travel)

pasajero (passenger)

ir a pie / caminar / andar (to walk)

transporte

el avión (plane)

el vuelo (flight)

el ferrocarril (railway)

You can download the specification containing the exam vocabulary list from the exam board website. Use this to learn the words on the Higher Tier list.

How confident do you feel about each of these **skills**? Colour in ✐ the bars.

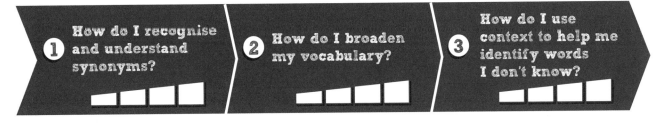

1 How do I recognise and understand synonyms?

2 How do I broaden my vocabulary?

3 How do I use context to help me identify words I don't know?

② Responding fully and correctly

This unit will help you to recognise the style of answer required and to respond in the correct way. The skills you will build are to:

- use clues in the question to shape your answer
- ensure you give complete answers
- consider specific detail demanded by a question.

In the exam you will be asked to do reading tasks similar to the ones on these two pages. This unit will prepare you to understand exactly what such questions are asking and to give full and correct answers.

Do not answer this exam-style question yet. You will be asked to at the end of the unit.

Exam-style question

Choosing a school

You read this leaflet about the San Lorenzo school.

> Para los padres, decidir cuál será el mejor instituto para vuestros hijos es un paso muy importante. En comun con la mayoría de los paises, la educación es obligatoria hasta los dieciséis años, por tanto, encontraréis una gran cantidad de institutos de educación secundaria públicos*. Por esta razón, nos gustaría tomar esta oportunidad de explicar porque pensamos que el Instituto San Lorenzo tiene las cualidades que buscáis.
>
> Estamos orgullosos de la variedad amplia de asignaturas que ofrecemos y, debido a las clases pequeñas, el estudiante recibirá atención individual por parte de los profesores. En términos de éxito escolar, el nivel es alto, y las notas se pueden ver en nuestra lista de resultados de exámenes.

Answer the questions in **English**.   *instituto público – state school*

Example What is an important step for parents?

Deciding which would be the best school for their children

1 What aspect of the education system is common to the majority of countries?   **(1 mark)**

2 What are they proud of at the school?   **(1 mark)**

3 What is the benefit of the small class sizes?   **(1 mark)**

4 Where could parents check the school's success rates?   **(1 mark)**

Questions are often written in a way that gives you a clue where to look for the answer.

(1) Read the exam-style question below. In the questions that follow the text, highlight the key words, which will guide you to the correct part of the text.

Do not answer this exam-style question yet. You will be asked to at the end of the unit.

Exam-style question

Exams

Your Spanish friend shows you this advice he has been reading about preparing for exams.

> En general, los exámenes le gustan a muy poca gente; aun los más estudiosos los encuentran estresantes. Lo mejor que se puede hacer para reducir esta ansiedad es prepararte bien y con tiempo.
>
> Mirar tus apuntes hasta el cansancio no sirve para nada; ante todo, el repaso tiene que ser activo. Podrías escribir resúmenes, anotar los apuntes con bolígrafos de color y buscar antiguos exámenes para practicar.
>
> Vale la pena diseñar un plan de repaso eficaz, dejando tiempo para todas las asignaturas y dándote tiempo de descanso también. Es importante relajarte y dormir bien además de estudiar. ¡Buena suerte!

Answer the questions in **English**.

Example   What is the general opinion of exams? *Few people like them*

1   How do the most studious students feel about exams?

....

(1 mark)

2   What is the best way to reduce anxiety when facing exams?

....

(1 mark)

3   What is the main recommendation for revision?

....

(1 mark)

4   What should a good revision plan allow time for?

....

(1 mark)

5   In addition to studying, what else must you do during the revision period?

....

(1 mark)

The three key questions in the **skills boosts** will help you recognise and understand core vocabulary, so you can respond fully and correctly.

 1 How do I use clues in the question to shape my answer?

2 How do I ensure that I give complete answers?

 3 How do I consider specific detail demanded by a question?

1 **How do I use clues in the question to shape my answer?**

The question title, introduction (which sets the scene) and the example answer (when one is given) all provide valuable information that you can use to your advantage.

(1) First look at the title of the exam-style question below, and the introductory sentence. In the word box, circle Ⓐ the vocabulary you might expect to see in the text. Then read the rest of the exam-style question, example answer and sample answers to questions **1–3**, and do the activities that follow.

estudiante	camarero	recreo	clases	fábrica	asistir	inundación
sin techo	intimidación	incendio	alumno	deportes	cine	participar

Exam-style question

El instituto

Ves este aporte en un foro sobre los aspectos de su instituto que los estudiantes quieren cambiar.

> En mi instituto, hay un gran problema con la cafetería. Durante el recreo, cientos de alumnos quieren comprar un bocadillo o una botella de agua pero las colas son enormes. Deben contratar a más personal y crear más cajas. También, para darnos más oportunidades de probar nuevos pasatiempos, creo que se debería ofrecer más actividades después de las clases. Por ejemplo, en el instituto de mi amigo inglés, se puede hacer teatro, participar en deportes o asistir al club de ajedrez. Quizás lo peor de todo es la intimidación que se ve en los pasillos y en el patio. Sin embargo los profesores controlan la situación bien y castigan a los culpables.

Contesta a las preguntas en **español**.

Ejemplo   ¿Cuál es el problema en el café? _Las colas son enormes._

1   ¿Qué soluciones ofrece para reducir las colas?

employ more staff and create more tills   **(1 mark)**

2   ¿Qué recomienda para dar más oportunidades de probar nuevos pasatiempos?

más actividades   **(1 mark)**

3   ¿Cómo responden los profesores al problema de la intimidación?

controlan bien la situación   **(1 mark)**

> From the title of the text, you know immediately the focus of the question and the range of topics and vocabulary that are likely to come up.

> Make sure you answer in the correct language.

(2) How would you describe the example answer above? Tick ✓ the three correct statements below.

In Spanish ☐   In English ☐

Full sentence ☐   Short statement ☐

Lifted from the text ☐

(3) Now look again at the sample answers to questions **1–3**. On paper, note down ✐ how each one is inappropriate compared to the example answer.

② How do I ensure that I give complete answers?

To give complete answers, it's important that you:

- read the questions carefully so you know exactly what is being asked of you. Make sure you understand question words in Spanish.
- scan the text to find the main area that contains the answer to the question
- read around the area to see if there is any other relevant information that will be required, or anything that contradicts what you've read.

Read the following text and questions in Spanish and do the activities that follow.

Una visita al instituto

Tu amigo mexicano, Alejandro, te muestra el artículo que ha escrito sobre su visita a tu instituto.

Es un <u>instituto</u> para alumnos de once a dieciséis años. Es mixto, como casi todos los institutos aquí. Asisten más de mil estudiantes y está situado en un barrio residencial de la pequeña ciudad. Todos los alumnos tienen un aspecto elegante porque llevan un uniforme azul. Además, tienen los zapatos bien limpios. ¡No son como los estudiantes mexicanos con sus vaqueros y zapatillas de deporte! Hay varias diferencias entre mi instituto y este, como la costumbre de llamar a los profesores por su apellido y comer en la enorme cantina del instituto. Quizás la diferencia más notable es el horario. ¡Los pobres no terminan hasta las tres y media! Una cosa que me ha gustado mucho es que, después de las clases, ofrecen una gran cantidad de actividades y deportes. Es un aspecto que tenemos que mejorar en mi propio instituto en México.

Contesta las preguntas en **español**.

1   ¿Para quiénes es el instituto?
2   ¿Cuántos estudiantes asisten al instituto?
3   ¿Por qué Alejandro piensa que son elegantes? Da dos razones.
4   ¿Qué llevan los alumnos en el instituto de Alejandro?
5   ¿Qué aspecto del horario no le gusta a Alejandro?
6   ¿Qué le gustaría ver en su propio instituto?

① First match up ✏️ the following question words in Spanish by drawing a line to their English equivalent.

A ¿Para quiénes?	a What?
B ¿Cuántos?	b Why?
C ¿Qué?	c How many?
D ¿Por qué?	d For whom?

② Now complete the following activities. In each case, the first question has been done for you.

a Highlight ✏️ the other key word or phrase in each question above.

b Then find and underline Ⓐ the same word or phrase in the text.

c Read the whole sentence containing the word(s) you have underlined and note down 📎 on paper whether it answers the question. If not, why not? For example:

It only answers the question partly. In the next sentence we learn that the school is mixed (mixto), so the school is for boys and girls between 11 and 16.

③ How do I consider specific detail demanded by a question?

The more challenging questions often require you to sift through information, reject what is not relevant and select only that which is needed in your answer. The question will hint at what you should be looking for.

① In the table below, read the short texts in Spanish and the questions in English about them. For each text:

- highlight 🖉 the key words in the question

- highlight 🖉 the section of the text that corresponds to the key word in the question

- cross out ~~cat~~ any of the text that is irrelevant

- in each 'Explanation' section, write 🖉 a sentence in English to explain how you chose the relevant section and why you rejected any parts that you crossed out.

The following words are often important in these types of questions: **más** – more, most; **mejor** – better, best; **menos** – less, least; **peor** – worse, worst

	Text	Question
a	~~En la Mezquita es importante quedarnos juntos en un grupo porque, si no, perderéis el comentario.~~ Lo esencial es mantener silencio.	What is it vital to do during the visit to the Mosque?
	Explanation: *'esencial' means 'vital' so links to this part of the text. The other instruction is important but not essential.*	
b	Después del inglés y la química, la informática suele ser la tercera asignatura más popular, según una encuesta reciente.	What is the most popular subject these days?
	Explanation:	
c	Cuando hace buen tiempo, suelo ir al instituto en bicicleta pero durante el invierno mi madre me lleva en el coche. Nunca voy a pie.	How does this student get to school in summer?
	Explanation:	
d	Dejé mis deberes de historia porque no entendí la tarea y acabo de terminar los ejercicios de matemáticas. Estoy a punto de hacer el ensayo para religión.	Which homework has this student completed?
	Explanation:	

Your turn!

Here is an exam-style question that requires you to put into practice the skills you have worked on, specifically using the information from the title, the introduction and the questions to inform your decision-making process. ✏️

Exam-style question

The importance of school

You are reading a Spanish magazine and see this article on the skills we develop at school.

> Desde el comienzo de la fase de enseñanza obligatoria, a los seis años, ir a la escuela nos da una enorme variedad de conocimientos y habilidades que no sabemos que estamos aprendiendo. Por primera vez tenemos que compartir los juguetes, los libros y, aun más importante, la atención de los mayores con numerosos otros niños. En cuanto a habilidades sociales, primero adquirimos la capacidad de escuchar a los otros y como consecuencia desarrollamos la tolerancia. En lo que se refiere a las habilidades de estudio, aprendemos a resolver problemas y, después, a persistir con una tarea hasta completarla. Cuando nos preguntan qué hemos aprendido en el instituto, siempre contestamos con una lista de asignaturas, pero en realidad el instituto nos da los requisitos para el trabajo y la vida en general.

Answer the questions in **English**.

Example   What begins at the age of six? *Compulsory education*

1   What is the most important thing we learn to share?

    .... (1 mark)

2   What social skill do we learn first?

    .... (1 mark)

3   What process skill do we develop second?

    .... (1 mark)

4   What do we *think* we learn in school?

    .... (1 mark)

5   What does school give us in addition?

    .... (1 mark)

Check the title to pinpoint the topic area. Note that the introductory sentence underneath specifically mentions 'skills'.

Remember to pay close attention to the example. What language are you answering in? What style is the answer?

Remember to consider key words like 'most', 'first' and 'second' in questions. Find the corresponding words in the text, as they will lead you to the right answer.

Your turn!

Here is an exam-style question that requires you to put into practice other skills you have worked on, specifically giving complete answers and providing specific detail. This time, the questions and answers are in Spanish. ✏️

Exam-style question

Problemas en el instituto

Ves estas cartas de estudiantes en una página de problemas en una revista española.

> El viernes que viene, hay una actividad solidaria en mi instituto y la idea de este evento, divertido para muchos, me da mucha ansiedad. Es un día de no uniforme y todos podemos llevar lo que queremos, si pagamos un euro cincuenta. Lo que pasa es que mi familia no tiene mucho dinero y no puedo competir con los ricos con su ropa y accesorios de marca. ¿Cómo puedo evitarlo?   *Alicia*

> Hace tres semanas, tuve una disputa con mi mejor amigo y nos peleamos porque él reveló un secreto mío a otras personas. Ahora me siento muy solo, y lo peor sería perder la amistad de Carlos para siempre. Al contrario, él ha encontrado a otros compañeros y los veo en el patio del instituto charlando y riéndose. ¿Cómo puedo recuperar esa amistad?   *Martín*

Contesta a las preguntas en **español**.

Ejemplo   ¿Qué tipo de evento va a celebrarse en el instituto de Alicia?

una actividad solidaria

1   ¿Qué emoción siente Alicia?

....

(1 mark)

2   ¿Cuánto cuesta participar en el evento?

....

(1 mark)

3   ¿Qué tienen 'los ricos' con lo que Alicia no puede competir?

....

(1 mark)

4   ¿Cuándo Martín se peleó con su amigo?

....

(1 mark)

5   ¿Qué sería lo peor para Martín?

....

(1 mark)

6   ¿Cómo ha reaccionado Carlos a perder la amistad de Martín?

....

(1 mark)

Don't fall into the trap of seeing the word *ropa* and giving just that as your answer. Keep reading and you'll find there is more to mention.

Remember that key words like *peor* will link to a specific part of the text. There may be other bad things happening to Martín, but what does he consider the worst?

The question wording can lead you to the detail required: for example, if the perfect tense is used in the question, look for it in the text to help you find the answer.

Review your skills

Check up

Review your responses to the exam-style questions on pages 15 and 16. Tick ✓ the column that shows how well you think you have done each of the following.

	Not quite ✓	Nearly there ✓	Got it! ✓
used clues in the question to shape my answer	☐	☐	☐
ensured that I gave a complete answer	☐	☐	☐
considered specific detail demanded by a question	☐	☐	☐

Need more practice?

Go back to pages 10 and 11 and complete ✏ the exam-style questions there. Use the checklist to help you. ✓

Checklist Before I answer the questions, have I ...	✓
paid close attention to the title, introduction and example answer provided?	
found all the relevant details in the text needed to fully answer the question?	
used the wording of the question to help me focus on the specific nature of the answer?	

Learn comparative and superlative adjectives with care, such as *más* (most), *mejor* (better) and *peor* (worst). Note down and learn other phrases and words that flag up specific sections of text: *sobre todo* – above all, *ante todo* – first of all and *más que nada* – more than anything.

How confident do you feel about each of these **skills**? Colour in ✏ the bars.

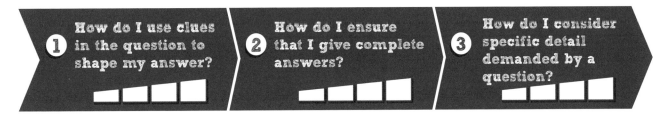

1 How do I use clues in the question to shape my answer?

2 How do I ensure that I give complete answers?

3 How do I consider specific detail demanded by a question?

③ Identifying relevant information

This unit will help you read the text with care, to eliminate irrelevant information and recognise details that are not true. The skills you will build are to:

- find the correct information in the text
- ensure you're not distracted by irrelevant information
- make sure you don't miss negatives.

In the exam, you will be asked to do reading tasks similar to the one on the opposite page. This unit will prepare you to tackle questions where it is important not to be misled by false or irrelevant information.

① Read the texts and questions in the exam-style question on page 19.

a In each of questions **1–5**, highlight ✐ one or two key words. Use a different colour for each question. Number one has been done for you.

b Now, using the same colour code, highlight ✐ one or two words in each of texts **A–G** that seem to relate to the words you highlighted in questions **1–5**. The first one has been done for you.

> Matching words from the questions to similar words in the text does sometimes help you find the correct information. But be careful: sometimes this can lead you astray – you must read the whole text to make sure you've understood the meaning fully.

Do not answer the exam-style question yet. You will be asked to at the end of the unit.

Exam-style question

Planes para el verano

Ves estos anuncios para eventos durante el verano en una red social española.

¿Cuál de los eventos es más apropiado para cada persona?

A	La estrella de la pequeña pantalla, Marta López, estará en la librería Santos el sábado 15 de julio para lanzar su nuevo libro, sobre su vida y experiencias.
B	El restaurante Castillo, sirviendo exclusivamente frutos del mar, tiene descuentos grandes en bacalao y merluza esta noche.
C	Los aficionados de la Copa Mundial disfrutarán del regreso de la selección nacional a la capital el sábado y de su vuelta de la ciudad en un autobús abierto.
D	Si quieres ver a tus actores y actrices favoritos en vivo, hay entradas para la grabación de la telenovela popular *La calle paralelo* este mes.
E	Concurso de pesca este fin de semana en el río Nalón: el ganador del torneo recibirá un premio de cien euros.
F	El autor célebre, Juan del Pozo, leerá extractos de su última novela *Naufragio* durante la Fiesta de la Lectura a principios de agosto.
G	Un programa de teatro para niños en el parque Paloma incluirá música, baile y canciones para entretener a los pequeños.

Escribe la letra correcta en cada casilla.

1 Me apetece marisco o pescado pero no tengo ganas de cocinar. ☐ (1 mark)

2 Me encantaría oírle recitar un capítulo de este libro. ☐ (1 mark)

3 Voy a dar la bienvenida a los jugadores que triunfaron en el torneo. ☐ (1 mark)

4 ¡Qué ilusión! Puedo conocer a mi actriz favorita de la tele. ☐ (1 mark)

5 Me encantaría ver una actuación en directo de un programa bien conocido. ☐ (1 mark)

The three key questions in the **skills boosts** will help you identify the information that is relevant to the question.

1 How do I ensure I find the correct information in the text?

2 How do I ensure I'm not distracted by irrelevant information?

3 How do I make sure I don't miss negatives?

1 **How do I ensure I find the correct information in the text?**

To find the correct information in a text, look carefully at what the question is asking. What tense is it in and who is it asking about? This will help you eliminate the incorrect information and find the right answer.

① Read the short texts below and the accompanying questions.

i Find the area of the text relevant to the question: underline (A) key words in both the question and the text.

> Remember to read around the area in the text to make sure you've not jumped at a false link.

ii Now cross out (cat) any part of the text that concerns a different subject or a different tense.

iii Answer (✏️) the questions, writing your answer in the space provided.

> Me encantaría ir al concierto contigo pero ~~mis padres salen al teatro esa noche~~ y <u>he prometido llevar a mi hermana a la pista de hielo</u>.   Andrea

> Does she go to the concert? No; she says she would love to but...
>
> Does she go to the theatre? No; it's her parents who are going to the theatre.
>
> Does she go to the ice rink? Yes; she is taking her sister there.

Example   <u>Where</u> is Andrea going? <u>ice rink</u>

> Perdí interés en los videojuegos de niño aunque Carlos piensa asistir, pero, sí tengo ganas de aprender el ajedrez. Quizás optaría por el debate si pudiera entender los eventos actuales en el mundo.   Iván

a Which club will Iván join? ....

> Me encanta la lectura. Antes insistía en leer los libros tradicionales pero ahora me he acostumbrado a usar una tableta, me parece más cómoda. Suelo confundirme con la trama cuando escucho los audiolibros.   Laura

b What does Laura prefer? ....

> En la escuela primaria era fanático del fútbol; luego, en la secundaria descubrí lo divertido que era el voleibol. Desde el año pasado, me entusiasmo por el baloncesto.   Gustavo

c What does Gustavo play? ....

2 **How do I ensure I'm not distracted by irrelevant information?**

You will need to read the text with care to spot phrases or vocabulary that can help you eliminate wrong information.

1 The box below contains Spanish words and phrases that are often used to show that information given is not actually true, and their English meanings. Draw lines 🖉 to match up the pairs. Look up any words that you don't know in a dictionary.

forbidden	mentir	to avoid	significar	evitar	to be mistaken	prohibido
to be right	tener razón	cierto	to lie	to mean	equivocarse	true

2 Read the Spanish sentences, and the questions and answer options that follow them. These sentences use Spanish vocabulary from the box above to indicate what is *not* a fact.

i In each sentence, highlight 🖉 the word or phrase that introduces incorrect information.

ii Now look again at the questions and answer options. Circle Ⓐ the correct answer.

Both options appear in the texts. It is only by understanding the whole sentence that you can rule out the wrong answer.

> Cuando vi a Pedro con Luisa, entendí que me había mentido cuando dijo que iba al fútbol.

Example What was Pedro doing?

Going to the football / (Going out with Luisa)

> Este mensaje no significa que no quiera salir contigo, simplemente que no tengo dinero para salir.

a What was the message?

He can't afford to go out. / He doesn't want to go out with her.

> Andrés se equivocó cuando dijo que la película empezó a las ocho. Ya son las ocho y todavía falta media hora.

b When does the film start?

Eight o'clock / Half past eight

> Oye, Carlos, no tienes razón en cuanto a Cristina. Es sevillana y tú estabas seguro de que era de Granada.

c Where is Cristina from?

Sevilla / Granada

> Siempre evitamos ir al cine los viernes porque hay demasiada gente. Solemos quedarnos en casa.

d What do they do on Fridays?

Go to the cinema / Stay at home

> ¿Has dicho que toco el piano? No es cierto. Mi instrumento es el teclado.

e What does he play?

Piano / Keyboard

> Quedamos en tomar un bocadillo en la playa ya que estaba prohibido hacer picnic en la hierba.

f What did they do for lunch?

Had a picnic on the grass / Had a sandwich on the beach

③ How do I make sure I don't miss negatives?

Remember to pay close attention to negative expressions when reading a text and when revising. Unless you recognise them, you may make the wrong assumption about a statement.

The sentence *No hay nada que me gusta más que dar un paseo en el campo* might seem negative because it includes *no* and *nada*, but the main message is positive: 'There is nothing I like better than walking in the country'. On the other hand, *El perro comió poco hoy* means 'the dog did not eat much today' (a negative comment), rather than the more positive 'the dog ate a little bit today'.

① Look at these negative words and phrases in context. Write 🖊 the English equivalent of the highlighted words.

a Es una lástima. Nadie quiere ir al concierto. ....

b Papá, ¿me das un poco de dinero? No tengo ninguno. ....

c No tengo nada que llevar para la fiesta. ....

d Para mi sorpresa, Mario no era español sino italiano. ....

e Jamás en mi vida he visto una película tan mala. ....

f Ya no me gusta ese libro; es un cuento de niños. ....

② Now look at the table below.

i For each Spanish statement, underline Ⓐ the negatives. That will ensure you don't miss any.

ii Then read the English summary and mark whether it is correct. ✓

iii Complete the table by writing 🖊 the reason for your decision.

Statement	Summary	✓	Reason
Example Iba a leer la novela hasta que consulté a mis amigos. <u>No les gustó a ningunos.</u>	I decided against reading the book.	✓	*It means 'I was going to read the book until I asked my friends. None of them liked it.'*
a Nada me pareció más hermosa que mi primera vista del mar a los siete años.	It was the best view I had seen.		
b Nadie tenía la menor idea de cuánto echaba de menos a mi familia esos primeros días.	I didn't really miss my family at first.		
c Solían decir que los niños no se interesaban en leer. Con los libros sobre el chico mágico, esto ya no es el caso.	Children aren't interested in reading any more.		
d Imagina mi vergüenza cuando descubrí que no había mandado el mensaje a Pablo sino a mi Papá.	She had sent the wrong message to her boyfriend.		

The writer says he <u>was going</u> to read the book until he learned that <u>none of his friends liked it</u>. We must conclude that he did not go on to read it.

Your turn!

Here is an exam style question that requires you to put into practice the skills that you have worked on, specifically identifying relevant information in the text and paying attention to negatives. 🖉

Exam-style question

Hobbies

You read this post by Daniela on a Spanish website about hobbies and pastimes.

> Yo creo que la gente confunde los pasatiempos sedentarios* con los pasivos. Es verdad que las actividades que me entusiasman a mí son físicamente poco activas. Pero esto no significa que soy una persona pasiva. Simplemente prefiero hacer cosas desafiantes para el cerebro en vez de para el cuerpo. Nunca hago deportes porque me faltan habilidades en eso; a mí me gustan más las actividades intelectuales. Me fascina el ajedrez, por ejemplo, y me encanta leer. Puede ser una afición un poco solitaria pero desarrollas la imaginación y siempre estás ampliando tu vocabulario. No es que sea una persona antisocial – paso todo el día relacionándome con otra gente en mi trabajo. Con un buen libro simplemente me gusta desconectar al final del día y perderme en la historia que estoy leyendo. ¡Me hace sufrir despedirme de mis personajes favoritos cuando llego al final!

*sedentario – sedentary, non-active

Underline the negative expressions in the text to ensure that you don't overlook any.

This is mentioned in the sentence after Daniela says she likes chess, but if you read on, you can work out which hobby she is referring to here.

1 Which **two** statements are true?

Write the correct letters in the boxes.

A	Daniela does not accept that her hobbies are passive ones.
B	She plays sport regularly.
C	She thinks that chess helps you develop your imagination.
D	She admits being a bit antisocial at times.
E	She has a lot of social interaction at work.

☐   ☐   **(2 marks)**

2 What does Daniela enjoy about a good book? Mention **two** things.

Answer in **English.**

1 ....

2 ....

(2 marks)

Your turn!

Here is an exam-style question that requires you to put in practice the skills you have worked on, specifically finding the correct information in a text and ensuring you are not distracted by irrelevant material. 🖉

Exam-style question

Families

You read this summary of the latest storyline in a Mexican soap opera.

> Los padres de Gabriela se divorciaron hace dos años y ahora la chica vive con su padre, Fernando, y su madrastra, Olga. Al principio Olga trataba a Gabriela con cariño pero ahora la chica entiende que era un acto para impresionar a su padre. Fernando piensa que su mujer es dulce y amable cuando lo contrario es verdad. Esa sonrisa suya no significa simpatía sino su intención de castigar a Gabriela cuando Fernando no está. También miente a Fernando diciendo que no tiene dinero, esperando que él se lo dé. Se compra ropa carísima y luego convence a su marido que es algo viejo que tiene desde hace años. También es cierto que ayer Gabriela la vio en el pueblo caminando con otro hombre. Fernando está muy equivocado cuando la describe como encantadora y leal. ¿Qué hará Gabriela en el próximo episodio?

Write the correct letter in each box.

1   What do we learn about the way Gabriela's stepmother treated her at first?

A	She was genuinely affectionate.
B	She treated her carefully, because of the divorce.
C	It was all for show.

☐

(1 mark)

2   How does she treat Gabriela now?

A	She is sweet and kind.
B	As if Gabriela were not significant.
C	It depends whether Gabriela's father is there or not.

☐

(1 mark)

3   How does Gabriela's stepmother get on with her new husband?

A	She is grateful to him for his generosity.
B	She lies to get money for fancy clothes.
C	She looks after him as he is much older than her.

☐

(1 mark)

4   What conclusion has Gabriela reached about her stepmother?

A	She is deceitful and unfaithful.
B	She is delightful and loyal.
C	She made a mistake and married the wrong man.

☐

(1 mark)

Look out for words like *pero* that may introduce a contrasting idea.

Although this is a near-cognate, you could miss it if you read the text too quickly.

This is a key phrase; if you miss this, you will misunderstand the whole sentence.

Make sure you learn *miente* or it may trip you up.

Review your skills

Check up

Review your responses to the exam-style questions on pages 23 and 24. Tick ✓ the column that shows how well you think you have done each of the following.

	Not quite ✓	Nearly there ✓	Got it! ✓
ensured I found the correct information in the text	☐	☐	☐
ensured I wasn't distracted by irrelevant information	☐	☐	☐
made sure I didn't miss negatives	☐	☐	☐

Need more practice?

Go back to page 19 and complete ✐ the exam-style question there. Use the checklist to help you. ✓

When answering the question on page 19, make sure you read around the key words you highlighted earlier to link the statements and text. Were any of the links you identified when you did ① ⓑ on page 18 misleading?

Checklist Before I answer the questions, have I...	✓
ensured that I read the text carefully so as not to make 'false links' based on a one-word match?	
recognised that there will be distracting information and eliminated it carefully?	
carefully looked at negative expressions to ensure I understand their meaning?	

How confident do you feel about each of these **skills**? Colour in ✐ the bars.

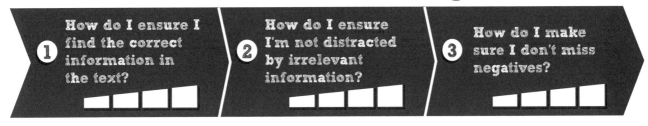

1. **How do I ensure I find the correct information in the text?**

2. **How do I ensure I'm not distracted by irrelevant information?**

3. **How do I make sure I don't miss negatives?**

④ Understanding a range of verbs and verbal structures

This unit will help you to recognise and develop your range of verbs and verbal structures. The skills you will build are to:

- use nouns and adjectives to broaden your range of verbs
- master less common or frequently confused verbs
- ensure you understand verbal structures.

In the exam, you will be asked to do reading tasks similar to the one on the opposite page. This unit will prepare you to focus on, recognise and understand a broader range of verbs.

① Look at the text in the exam-style question on the opposite page. Each highlighted verb is related to a similar noun or adjective. Recognising these similarities can help you to understand the verb.

Decide which of the nouns and adjectives in the box below match the verbs in the text. Complete ✐ the table to record the adjective/noun, the related verb form in the text and the infinitive of the verb and its likely meaning.

> *aburrido* – bored/boring   *alegre* – cheerful, happy   *decepcionante* – disappointing
>
> *entretenido* – entertaining   *helado / hielo* – ice cream / ice

Adjective / Noun	Verb form in the text	Infinitive form	Meaning
aburrido			
alegre			
decepcionante			
entretenido			
helado/hielo			

Do not answer the exam-style question yet. You will be asked to at the end of the unit.

Exam-style question

Sport

You read Mario's blogpost about football.

> Aquí Mario. Yo soy un fanático del fútbol pero hay días cuando no sé por qué. Hay partidos que me aburren un montón, como el fin de semana pasado cuando el viento me heló y, más que nada, la falta de goles me decepcionó. Sin embargo, en otras ocasiones, me alegra el ambiente en el estadio y me divierte estar en la compañía de mis amigos. No es solo el fútbol que es capaz de entretener a millones de aficionados cada semana. Me sorprendió mucho este hecho: que uno de los deportes de mayor popularidad en España es la pesca. Cuando les dije a mis amigos pescadores que no me interesa nada, me aseguraron* de que es una actividad fascinante.

*asegurar – to assure

The highlighted verb *aburren* is linked to *aburrido* (bored/boring) and *aburrimiento* (boredom). From this, you can deduce that *aburrir* means 'to bore'.

Answer the questions in **English**.

1   What **exactly** were the weather conditions at last weekend's match?

    ....

    (1 mark)

2   What was Mario's main reaction to the match?

    ....

    (1 mark)

3   How does Mario react to being at the football ground? Mention **two** things.

    1   ....

    2   ....

    (2 marks)

4   What did Mario learn about fishing and how did he react to the information?

    ....

    (1 mark)

5   What did his friends do when he told them his opinion of fishing?

    ....

    (1 mark)

The three key questions in the **skills boosts** will help you understand a range of verbs and verbal structures.

 1 How do I use nouns and adjectives to broaden my range of verbs?

 2 How do I master less common or frequently confused verbs?

 3 How do I ensure I understand verbal structures?

1 How do I use nouns and adjectives to broaden my range of verbs?

Many verbs, whether in English or Spanish, are related to similar nouns and adjectives that share the same root. You can learn these as 'families' of words, using cards to record and learn them.

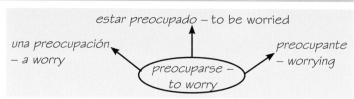

estar preocupado – to be worried

una preocupación – a worry

preocuparse – to worry

preocupante – worrying

1 i Underline Ⓐ the noun in the Spanish phrases below. Do you know any verbs that contain this word or part of it? They are all –ar verbs.

ii On paper, write down ✏ the verbs and their English meaning.

Example causar <u>intimidación</u> = <u>intimidar – to bully, intimidate</u>

- **a** dar apoyo
- **b** servir como guía
- **c** hacer una pregunta
- **d** dar una explicación
- **e** hacer un dibujo
- **f** hacer una grabación
- **g** dar empleo
- **h** tener un fracaso
- **i** hacer un diseño
- **j** ser molesto

2 Study the Spanish nouns and adjectives and their English equivalents in the word box below. Then, cover up the word box and circle Ⓐ the correct meaning of the underlined verb in the Spanish sentences.

> cansado – tired   contenedor – container   lleno – full   parada de autobús – bus stop
>
> queja – complaint   retraso – delay   robo – theft / robbery   solución – solution

- **a** El tren <u>paró</u> en la estación.
  arrived / left / stopped

- **b** Alguien había <u>robado</u> el collar.
  stolen / found / bought

- **c** He <u>solucionado</u> el problema.
  discovered / solved / explained

- **d** El atasco me <u>retrasó</u>.
  infuriated / delayed / worried

- **e** Tengo que <u>rellenar</u> los detalles.
  read / learn / fill in

- **f** Este folleto <u>contiene</u> la información.
  translates / provides / contains

- **g** El ejercicio me <u>cansó</u>.
  tired / confused / helped

- **h** El cliente <u>se quejó</u>.
  complained / gave a tip / left

> Now that you are familiar with the verbs in **2**, look up the infinitive of each one and record it along with its meaning. Build a word family by adding the related noun or adjective from **2**. For example: *cansar – to tire   cansado – tired*

2 **How do I master less common or frequently confused verbs?**

There is no substitute for learning vocabulary, but this page will help you build your knowledge and use and practise a range of verbs. Some of these are frequently confused and others are not seen as often.

1 **a** The box below contains Spanish verbs that are frequently confused, and their meanings. Draw lines (✐) to match up each Spanish verb with its English equivalent.

Try out various vocabulary-learning strategies, like asking a friend to test you or using a vocabulary-learning website. Find out what works best for you.

pedir	to take / carry / wear	perder	poder	to arrive	to be able
llevar	to ask for	lavar	to lose	levantarse	llegar	to wash	to get up

b Circle (Ⓐ) the verb that is most appropriate in sentences **i–viii** below.

i   Los fines de semana me llevo / llego / levanto tarde.

ii   El equipo pidió / perdió / pudo el partido tres a cero.

iii   Mis abuelos llevaron / llegaron / lavaron ayer.

iv   Con el deporte puedes / pierdes / pides hacer más amigos.

v   Mi hermana llegaba / lavaba / llevaba un hermoso vestido blanco.

vi   Tengo que pedir / poder / perder ayuda con estos deberes.

vii   Gano dinero el sábado llegando / llevando / lavando el coche.

viii Creo que he perdido / pedido / podido mis llaves.

Create a mnemonic (memory trick) to help you remember verbs you often confuse. It could be a silly sentence like *Si pides ayuda, no puedes perder*. (If you ask for help, you cannot lose).

2 **a** The verbs in the word box below are synonyms for the verbs in column A of the table. In general, the verbs in column A are more commonly used than the ones in the box. Select the correct synonym from the box and write it (✐) in column B next to the appropriate verb.

b Then complete the table: write down (✐) the meaning of the verb in English.

Many of the verbs on the GCSE vocabulary list have a less well-known synonym also on the list. It is a good idea to learn them in pairs.

A broad knowledge of synonyms will help you to recognise less common verbs and, therefore, to better understand more challenging texts.

caminar	desear	echar	empezar	enseñar
enviar	fastidiar	ocurrir		

A	B	Meaning
comenzar		
andar		
tirar		
pasar		
querer		
molestar		
mandar		
mostrar		

3 **How do I ensure I understand verbal structures?**

The verbs on this page are more complex than the verbs seen earlier in the unit as they consist of more than one word and often differ in meaning from the core verb. For example, *acabar* on its own means 'to finish / to end', but *acabar de* + infinitive means 'to have just...'.

1 Read the following sentences and, using the context, choose the correct meaning of the verb from the word box. Write 🖉 the meaning in the space provided.

Word box
to be worth (it)
to continue to...
to feel like
to have just...
to start to
to stop ...ing
to tend to

a No vale la pena ir a la biblioteca porque se cierra en diez minutos.

(valer la pena = ...)

b Mi hermana se pone a llorar cuando ve una película triste.

(ponerse a + infinitive = ...)

c Estoy un poco cansada, no tengo ganas de salir.

(tener ganas de = ...)

d Mi padre dice que dejará de fumar este verano.

(dejar de + infinitive = ...)

e No he visto a Pablo porque acabo de llegar.

(acabar de + infinitive = ...)

f Los sábados suelo ir al fútbol con mi padre.

(soler + infinitive = ...)

g Hacía muy mal tiempo y siguió lloviendo.

(seguir + present participle = ...)

2 For each Spanish sentence below, three options are given for the meaning of the verb. Circle Ⓐ the correct option, and write 🖉 the infinitive of the verb in your vocabulary list.

a Acabo de verlo.

　　A I have just seen it　　　B It was worth seeing it　　　C I felt like seeing it

b Tiene ganas de dormir.

　　A he slept again　　　B he feels like sleeping　　　C he continued to sleep

c Vale la pena ir.

　　A I felt like going　　　B I stopped going　　　C It's worthwhile going

d Siguió andando.

　　A he carried on walking　　　B he stopped walking　　　C he felt like walking

e Suele ayudar.

　　A she starts to help　　　B she agrees to help　　　C she tends to help

f Se puso a escribir.

　　A he wrote again　　　B he stopped writing　　　C he started to write

g Dejó de nevar.

　　A it stopped snowing　　　B it continued to snow　　　C it snowed again

Your turn!

Here is an exam-style question that requires you to put into practice the skills you have worked on, specifically recognising and understanding verbs you came across earlier in this unit. 🖊

Exam-style question

Carlos Acosta

You read this article about the dancer, Carlos Acosta, on a Cuban website about role models.

> En una entrevista grabada en febrero, Carlos Acosta explicó que empezó a ir a clases de ballet porque su padre opinaba que serían buenas para su disciplina. Al principio, no deseaba participar y se quejaba cada semana, pero su padre siguió enviándole a la escuela de baile. Poco a poco iba descubriendo un talento natural para la danza. Guiado y apoyado por sus profesores, Acosta se puso a tomar el ballet en serio y comenzó a soñar con un futuro como bailarín.
>
> El éxito internacional llegó cuando ganó la medalla de oro en el prestigioso Prix de Lausanne, en Suiza, y Acosta luego bailó con las principales compañías de ballet del mundo. Para él, lo más difícil siempre ha sido la soledad que ha experimentado. Echó de menos a su familia, y, después de casarse, le fastidiaba separarse de su mujer y de su hija. Acepta que cuando se escoge una carrera que implica tours y actuaciones internacionales, hay problemas que no se pueden solucionar.
>
> Acosta ha mostrado al mundo que su capacidad creativa no se limita al baile. Ha escrito una novela, además de su autobiografía, y ha diseñado coreografía para varias producciones. Es un hombre que no se cansa nunca y que no tiene intención de parar.

Answer the questions in **English.**

1 Why did Acosta start having ballet lessons?

....
(1 mark)

2 How did Acosta react to the lessons at first?

....
(1 mark)

3 What encouraged Acosta to take ballet seriously?

....
(1 mark)

4 What made Acosta feel lonely at times?

....
(1 mark)

5 In addition to writing, in what other creative role has Acosta been involved?

....
(1 mark)

Se quejaba – la queja means 'a complaint', so use that to work out the meaning of this verb

Se puso a – you learned *ponerse a* earlier in the unit – do you remember what it meant?

Fastidiaba – you met this verb earlier in the unit as a synonym of another verb. Do you remember that other verb?

Diseñado – do you know any nouns related to this verb? Note them down alongside the infinitive of this past participle.

Your turn!

Here is an exam-style question that requires you to put into practice the skills you have worked on, specifically understanding a range of verbs and verbal structures.

Exam-style question

A quiz

Your Spanish friend, Jorge, has answered this questionnaire from a magazine. Look at the answers he has circled.

¿Eres un adolescente perezoso?

¿Eres un típico joven vago o sacas mucho provecho de tu tiempo libre? Haz este test y descubre la verdad sobre tu personalidad. Puedes ver los resultados en la página 48.

Ejemplo Hay una exhibición sobre pasatiempos diferentes en tu instituto. ¿Vas a ir?

- **(A)** Estaré allí cuando se abra la puerta.
- **(B)** No me da la gana.
- **C** Si tengo tiempo

1 Son las ocho de la mañana el domingo. ¿Qué haces?

- **(A)** Estoy haciendo footing en el parque.
- **B** Sigo durmiendo.
- **(C)** Acabo de levantarme.

2 Dicen que van a cerrar la biblioteca en el pueblo. ¿Cómo respondes?

- **A** La voy a echar muy de menos.
- **B** ¿Biblioteca? ¿Dónde está?
- **C** Usaré el ordenador.

3 Descubres que has pasado dos horas jugando un videojuego. ¿Qué haces?

- **A** Dejo de jugar en seguida.
- **B** Sigo jugando dos horas más.
- **C** No pierdo mi tiempo jugando videojuegos.

You must learn key verbal structures like *acabar de*, as these can be hard to work out from the context but may change the meaning of a sentence.

Answer the questions in **English**. Tick the correct box.

Example Does Jorge have a positive reaction to trying new things?

Yes [ ] No [✓] Give a reason for your answer.

He can't be bothered to go to an exhibition at school about different hobbies

Notice that with this type of question you have to summarise the quiz question as well as the circled answer.

1 Do you think that Jorge is lazy at the weekend?

Yes [ ] No [ ] Give a reason for your answer.

.... (1 mark)

2 Do you think that Jorge makes the most of local facilities?

Yes [ ] No [ ] Give a reason for your answer.

.... (1 mark)

3 Does Jorge try to avoid wasting time?

Yes [ ] No [ ] Give a reason for your answer.

.... (1 mark)

Review your skills

Check up

Review your responses to the exam-style questions on pages 31 and 32. Tick ✓ the column that shows how well you think you have done each of the following.

	Not quite ✓	Nearly there ✓	Got it! ✓
used nouns and adjectives to broaden my range of verbs	☐	☐	☐
mastered less common or frequently confused verbs	☐	☐	☐
understood verbal structures	☐	☐	☐

Need more practice?

Go back to page 27 and complete ✏ the exam-style question there. Use the checklist to help you. ✓

Checklist Before I answer the questions, have I...	✓
used nouns and adjectives to help me work out the meaning of verbs?	
mastered less common or frequently confused verbs?	
studied the verbal structures explored in Skills boost 3?	

Also learn these useful verbs from the Higher Tier vocabulary list:

despedirse de – to say goodbye to

disculparse – to apologise

esforzarse – to make an effort

parecerse a – to look like, resemble

relacionarse con – to relate to

hacer cola – to queue

ocuparse de – to look after.

How confident do you feel about each of these **skills**? Colour in ✏ the bars.

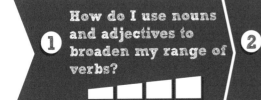
1. How do I use nouns and adjectives to broaden my range of verbs?

2. How do I master less common or frequently confused verbs?

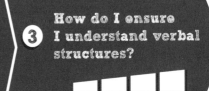
3. How do I ensure I understand verbal structures?

⑤ Recognising and understanding grammatical clues

This unit will help you to recognise and better understand aspects of grammar that are important in reading comprehension. The skills you will build are to:

- recognise which tense verbs are in
- make the most of time phrases found in the texts
- recognise the subject of the verb and any object pronouns.

In the exam, you will be asked to do reading tasks similar to the one on this page. This unit will help you to use tenses and time phrases to locate the correct answer, and to differentiate between the subject and the object of a verb.

Look at the exam-style question below and do the activities that follow. Do not answer the exam-style question yet. You will be asked to at the end of the unit.

Exam-style question

Holidays

You read this Spanish magazine article about Jacinto and Aurora Jiménez and their holidays.

> Los Jiménez son un matrimonio muy feliz que llevan 18 años casados pero que raramente van de vacaciones juntos. "Es que tenemos preferencias muy diferentes" declara Jacinto "y nos conviene mucho mejor así". Hace un año, Aurora pasó una semana en los Alpes, esquiando y disfrutando el aire puro de las montañas, En cambio, su marido estuvo siete días cerca de Edimburgo: "fui a hacer senderismo y a pescar en los ríos escoceses", explica Jacinto. De momento, la señora Jiménez está visitando las ruinas romanas en Italia mientras que su marido se divierte en un crucero en el Caribe. Sin embargo, el abril que viene se encontrarán los dos en safari en África. "Es la única cosa que nos interesa a los dos," dice Aurora, riéndose.

What time period applies to the following holidays mentioned by Jacinto and Aurora Jiménez?

Write **P** for something that happened in the **past**.

Write **N** for something that is happening **now**.

Write **F** for something that is going to happen in the **future**.

Write the correct letter in each box.

1	A sporty winter holiday	(1 mark)
2	An active holiday in the countryside	(1 mark)
3	A tropical holiday at sea	(1 mark)
4	Seeing animals in the wild	(1 mark)
5	Visiting the remains of ancient civilizations	(1 mark)

1 In the text in the exam-style question on page 34:

The time phrases and verbs will be important when you come back to answer the exam-style question at the end of the unit.

a circle (A) any time phrases that indicate when the events are happening

b underline (A) the verbs in tenses that indicate when holidays are taking place.

In this unit you will be using four main tenses: the preterite, the imperfect, the future and the near future. Here you will focus on the regular forms of these tenses.

Refer to your text book if you need to revise the preterite, imperfect, future and near future tenses.

2 The sentences below feature the future and the near future. Translate (✎) each one into English, on paper. Remember: the future translates 'will…' and the near future conveys 'to be going to…'.

a Aparcaré el coche aquí.

b Vamos a comprar billetes de ida y vuelta.

c ¿Vas a ir en barco?

d Dejaremos las maletas en la consigna.

e Voy a quejarme del ruido.

f El tren pronto va a detenerse en la estación.

g Os divertiréis en Málaga.

h Los niños volverán a la piscina esta tarde.

3 In the text below most of the verbs are in the preterite and the imperfect.

Be careful of the common irregular forms in the text: *iban, era, estuve* and *fue*.

a Underline (A) all the examples of these tenses.

b Write (✎) the verbs into the correct column, noting which person they are in (I = 1ps; you = 2ps; he/she/it = 3ps; we = 1pp; you plural = 2pp, they = 3pp).

c Complete your table by translating (✎) the verbs into English.

Hace unos años, los Jiménez iban de vacaciones juntos pero las cosas no salían bien. "Una vez, pasamos una semana en un barco navegando los canales de Inglaterra. Estuve muy aburrida y el viaje fue lentísimo" explica Aurora. "Pero Jacinto disfrutó de la tranquilidad y pensó que el campo era precioso". Cuando viajaban juntos, no podían encontrar vacaciones que les gustaban a los dos. "Teníamos muchas disputas hasta que un día resolvimos el problema y ¡decidimos ir de vacaciones separadamente!" afirma Jacinto.

Preterite	English translation	Imperfect	English translation
pasamos (1pp)	we spent		

The three key questions in the **skills boosts** will help you recognise and understand grammatical clues.

1 How do I recognise which tense verbs are in?

2 How do I make the most of time phrases in the texts?

3 How do I recognise the subject of the verb and any object pronouns?

1 How do I recognise which tense verbs are in?

Some comprehension questions test your recognition and understanding of the different tenses, so it is essential to know them thoroughly.

(1) Events in the future will usually be in either the future or the near future tense. Highlight ✏ the examples of these tenses in the following sentences, using a different colour for each tense. (Be careful, there are verbs in other tenses as well.)

> Refer to your text book if you need to revise the future and near future tenses.

a El sábado fuimos a la playa pero el lunes vamos a pasar el día en el parque acuático.

b En mayo habrá una fiesta porque es el día del santo patrón del pueblo.

c Compré este recuerdo pero voy a devolverlo porque está roto.

d Tuvimos mucha suerte con el tiempo pero creo que lloverá pronto.

e Voy a mirar los detalles ahora y reservaré el hotel mañana.

(2) The most commonly used past tenses are the preterite and the imperfect. Translate ✏ the sentences below, ensuring you convey the sense of the preterite or imperfect accurately.

> The preterite conveys completed, 'one-off' actions or events and is usually translated in English by the simple past: 'saw', found', 'made', and so on. The imperfect deals with ongoing or repeated actions and is translated by 'was/were … -ing' or 'used to…'

a Solo visité México una vez. ....

b Cada año comíamos en el mismo restaurante. ....

c Pasábamos las mañanas en la playa. ....

d Mis padres alquilaron un coche. ....

e Cuando esquiaba en Italia, me rompí la pierna. ....

(3) The following text, written by Paula, features verbs in five different tenses.

a Circle ⓐ the verbs in the present tense.

b Underline Ⓐ the verbs in the near future tense.

c Highlight ✏ the verbs in the future, preterite and imperfect tenses, using a different colour for each tense.

> Prefiero ir al extranjero cuando voy de vacaciones porque en general hace más calor. De pequeño, no prestaba mucha atención al tiempo porque siempre lo pasaba bien jugando en la playa. Recuerdo un día cuando mis padres tuvieron que arrastrarme* de la playa porque había una tormenta enorme. Ahora el sol me importa más y sobre todo la semana próxima porque vamos a estar en Lanzarote. El pronóstico dice que hará buen tiempo aparte de miércoles cuando va a haber viento.

*arrastrar – to drag

(4) Now look at the questions on the text. Annotate ✏ the five tenses in the same way as you did with the text in (3). This will narrow down which part of the text the answer must come from.

a ¿Por qué Paula prefiere ir al extranjero de vacaciones?

b Cuando Paula era pequeña, ¿cómo reaccionaba al tiempo?

c ¿Qué hicieron sus padres el día de la gran tormenta?

d ¿Qué van a hacer la semana que viene?

e ¿Por qué no van a ir a la playa el miércoles?

2 How do I make the most of time phrases in the texts?

Often, the tense of the verb is supported by a time phrase or word that gives a further clue to when an event is taking place. It is important to learn these and to spot them when reading a text.

1 Look at this table containing Spanish time words / phrases.

a Write ✎ the English for those that you know, and look up any that you don't.

b In the far-right column, write ✎ **P** if the word / phrase refers to the past, **N** if it refers to now and **F** if it refers to the future.

Spanish	English	P/N/F
de momento		
pasado mañana		
anteayer		
dentro de tres días		

Spanish	English	P/N/F
hace una semana		
esta noche		
anoche		
en el porvenir		

2 Read the following text, then:

a circle Ⓐ the time phrases (not just those from in the list above)

b draw an arrow ✎ between each time phrase and the verb that it is referring to

c note down ✎ the tense of the verb above each one.

> Hace un siglo, Benidorm era un pequeño pueblo de pescadores y, en esos días, no tenía visitantes.
>
> Se convirtió en una ciudad turística durante los años setenta, haciéndose famosa por sus enormes hoteles y millones de veraneantes. En este momento la ciudad está tratando de recuperar su identidad española y, en los meses que vienen, hay planes de mejorar los parques y jardines. La semana próxima, se abrirá el nuevo paseo marítimo.

3 Now read the sentences below. Each one contains three time-phrase options.

Make sure you know the meanings of all the time phrases listed here.

i Highlight ✎ the verb in each sentence and decide what tense it is in.

ii Then, underline Ⓐ the correct time phrase / word in each sentence.

a Ayer / Dentro de dos días / De momento no puedo llamar el hotel porque estoy ocupado.

b Pasado mañana / Anoche / Mañana decidimos no salir e hicimos una cena en el apartamento.

c A partir de mañana / Anoche / Anteayer voy a empezar a ahorrar para las vacaciones.

d El sábado que viene / Todos los sábados / El sábado pasado estaré en Valencia.

e En un concurso hace tres meses / ahora / en el porvenir mis padres ganaron un fin de semana en Málaga.

③ How do I recognise the subject of the verb and any object pronouns?

You need to focus on the verb ending in Spanish to know who or what the subject is (that is, who or what is doing the action of the verb). Do not look at an object pronoun and confuse it with the subject.

① Carry out the following on the Spanish sentences below using the example as a guide.

Object pronouns: *me* (me/to me), *te* (you/to you), *lo* (it, masc.), *la* (her/it, fem.) *le* (to him/to her), *nos* (us/to us), *os* (you, plural / to you, plural), *los* (them, masc), *las* (them, fem), *les* (to them)

i   Identify and write down 🖉 which person of the verb is being used.

ii   Find and write down 🖉 the subject of the verb.

iii   Identify the object pronoun in front of the verb: write it down 🖉 with its meaning.

iv   Translate 🖉 the sentence into English.

Example Mi padre es muy generoso; me dio dinero para mis vacaciones.

The word order will help you: *dio* is the verb 'he/she/it gave'. The *me*, which comes in front of the verb, tells us who the person (subject) gave the money to.

> *dio: he/she/it (3rd person singular)* subject: *father*
>
> object pronoun: *me = me*
>
> translation: *My father is very generous; he gave me money for my holidays.*

a A mi abuela le gustan los recuerdos y le compré un abanico en la tienda.

> *compré:* .... subject: .... object pronoun: ....
>
> translation: ....

b Tu novia te manda un mensaje todos los días, ¿verdad?

> *manda:* .... subject: .... object pronoun: ....
>
> translation: ....

c Los niños hacían mucho ruido y una señora anciana les gritó.

> *gritó:* .... subject: .... object pronoun: ....
>
> translation: ....

② Look at the following sentences in English and Spanish, focusing on the verb ending and the object pronoun in front of the verb. Circle Ⓐ the correct Spanish translation.

a | I found them on the floor.

Me encontraron en el suelo. / Las encontré en el suelo. / Me encontré en el suelo.

b | He explained the problem to us.

Nos explicó el problema. / Le explicamos el problema. / Nos explicamos el problema.

c | I'll send you the photos.

Me mandaré las fotos. / Te mandaré las fotos. / Te mandarás las fotos.

Your turn!

Here is an exam-style question that will help you to put into practice the skills you have learned, specifically recognising and understanding the tenses and time phrases. It will also allow you to check your grasp of the subject and object of a verb.

(1) Read the exam-style question below.

a In the text, to make sure you've understood the different tenses, use different colours or patterns to underline (A) examples of the imperfect tense, preterite, future tense, near future tense and any time phrases.

b Underline (A) the verbs in questions **1–6** of the exam-style question using the same system you used for the text. This tense/time phrase recognition tool will help you find the information you need.

(2) Now translate this phrase from the text: *la recepcionista está tratándonos muy bien y la compañía me va a dar una recompensa.* Look at the verb endings to find the subject of the verb.

....

....

Exam-style question

Vacaciones decepcionantes

Lees este correo electrónico de tus amigos españoles que tienen problemas con su apartamento.

> Durante todo el año nos sentíamos muy emocionados por la idea de pasar las vacaciones en la costa del sur de Portugal y teníamos muchas ideas sobre lo que íbamos a hacer y las cosas que queríamos ver. Todo eso cambió esta mañana al llegar al apartamento. Todo estaba sucio y las ventanas daban a un aparcamiento. Además, estaba mucho más lejos de la playa de lo que decía en el sitio web. Fuimos en seguida a la recepción para quejarnos.
>
> De momento estamos esperando en la recepción porque van a encontrarnos habitaciones en un hotel para la noche. Dice que mañana por la tarde tendrán un apartamento libre que tiene vistas al mar. Para ser honesto, la recepcionista está tratándonos muy bien y la compañía me va a dar una recompensa.

Contesta las preguntas en **español**.

1 ¿Cómo se sentían los Sánchez antes de ir de vacaciones? **(1 mark)**

....

2 ¿Por qué no estaban contentos con la condición del apartamento? **(1 mark)**

....

3 ¿Qué problema había con la situación del apartamento? **(1 mark)**

....

4 ¿Adónde fueron para quejarse? **(1 mark)**

....

5 ¿Dónde van a pasar esta noche? **(1 mark)**

....

6 ¿Cuándo tendrán un apartamento adecuado? **(1 mark)**

....

Your turn!

Use the skills you have developed to tackle this exam-style question. The tenses and time phrases will provide key clues in answering the questions.

Exam-style question

Travels abroad

You receive an email from your Spanish friend who has travelled to Canada on an adventure holiday.

> ¡Hola!
>
> Aquí lo pasamos bomba y cada día es una aventura. Hoy nos ocurrió que durante el viaje hemos probado casi todos los tipos de transporte que existen. Esta tarde vamos a coger el tren histórico que solía transportar a los mineros cuando iban a las minas de oro. Anteayer, fuimos en helicóptero a un glaciar para ver los perros de trineo* en su campamento en la nieve. De momento, claro, estamos a bordo el gran barco *La Princesa* haciendo un crucero y cada día desembarcamos para visitar algún sitio o hacer actividades. Dentro de dos días estaremos haciendo piragüismo en un lago mientras que hace tres días estuvimos en un viejo carruaje tirado por dos grandes caballos. Todo es fantástico, ¡un sueño hecho realidad!

trineo – sleigh/sledge

Which period of time applies to the activities described by your friend?

Write **P** for something that happened in the **past**.

Write **N** for something that is happening **now**.

Write **F** for something that is going to happen in the **future**.

Write the correct letter in each box.

1	A canoe trip	(1 mark)
2	A cruise	(1 mark)
3	A sleigh ride	(1 mark)
4	Horse and carriage ride	(1 mark)
5	A railway journey	(1 mark)

You can start by using the vocabulary in the question to locate the relevant sentence in the text. For instance 'horse and carriage' in question 4 will lead you to *caballos*. Then you can focus on the verbs and the time phrases in the sentence to pinpoint when the activity took place.

Review your skills

Check up

Review your responses to the exam-style questions on pages 39 and 40. Tick ✓ the column that shows how well you think you have done each of the following.

	Not quite ✓	Nearly there ✓	Got it! ✓
recognised which tense verbs are in	☐	☐	☐
made the most of time phrases in the text	☐	☐	☐
recognised the subject of the verb and any object pronouns	☐	☐	☐

Need more practice?

Go back to page 34 and complete ✏ exam-style question there. Use the checklist to help you. ✓

Checklist Before I answer the questions, have I...	✓
used my knowledge of tenses to understand both the questions and the text?	
looked at the time phrases and used them to inform my answer?	
used the verb ending to work out the subject of the verb, not confusing it with the object pronoun?	

How confident do you feel about each of these **skills**? Colour in ✏ the bars.

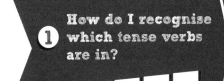

1 How do I recognise which tense verbs are in?

2 How do I make the most of time phrases in the texts?

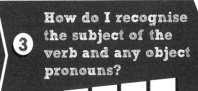

3 How do I recognise the subject of the verb and any object pronouns?

⑥ Inferring meaning

This unit will help you infer meaning from what is written in a text. The skills you will build are to:

- infer positive and negative ideas
- infer opinion and justification
- infer meaning by combining information from different parts of a text.

In the exam you will be asked to do reading tasks similar to the ones on these two pages. This unit will prepare you to infer meaning from the information given in the text.

When someone expresses opinions, it is often useful to look at the connective that joins their opinions. Look at the two highlighted connectives in the passage below. Think about whether each of these indicates a similar opinion (*Es bonito y barato*), or a contradiction (*Es bonito pero caro*). A contradictory connective often indicates that positive and negative opinions are being expressed.

Do not answer this exam-style question yet. You will be asked to at the end of the unit.

Exam-style question

Una fiesta loca

Read Enrique's account of his visit to the Tomatina.

El pueblo de Buñol, donde se celebra la famosa fiesta de los tomates, es un pueblo normal, bastante feo para ser honesto, y sin gran atractivo cultural. Cuando llegué, ya había bastante gente y al principio pensé que no iba a poder encontrar un hotel. Afortunadamente, un hostal había tenido una cancelación y me alojé allí, contento de haber encontrado una habitación cómoda, limpia y, además, idealmente situada. La fiesta misma era exactamente cómo había leído: una hora loca de risa y diversión cuando hablé con jóvenes encantadores de todas las naciones del mundo. Lo pasé la mar de bien.* Al final, cubierto de tomate y terriblemente sucio, intenté lavarme en las duchas comunales. Esto era lo peor porque no había sitio para todos y tuvimos que hacer cola largo rato. Sin embargo, funcionaban bien y la sensación de estar limpio fue un gran placer.

*pasarlo la mar de bien – to have a really good time

How did Enrique feel about the following? Write **P** (Positive), **N** (Negative) or **P+N** (Positive and Negative).

1 The town of Buñol   ☐ (1 mark)

2 His hotel room   ☐ (1 mark)

3 The festival itself   ☐ (1 mark)

4 The showers   ☐ (1 mark)

You need to ensure you consider all the opinions, even when they are in a different part of the text.

① Read the sentences below.

Mi hijo Leo es adicto a su móvil.	Cuando voy por la ciudad el aire no es puro.
Malgasta tanto tiempo mirando la pantalla.	Es refrescante correr en el parque.
Encuentro la lectura muy relajante.	Leo sobre todo novelas de fantasía.

a Group the sentences into three overall topics. Underline Ⓐ the sentences that discuss jogging. Circle Ⓐ sentences about reading and highlight ✏ sentences about mobile phones.

b Decide whether the overall opinion of the topic is positive, negative or positive and negative. Write ✏ P, N or P+N in the relevant box.

Jogging ☐ Reading ☐ Mobile phones ☐

Do not answer the exam-style question yet. You will be asked to at the end of the unit.

Exam-style question

Hobby day

Read this account of when Roberto tried out some new activities at school.

Hoy hemos tenido la oportunidad en el instituto de probar algunos nuevos pasatiempos. Empecé con un partido de voleibol que no he jugado antes y descubrí que tenía un poco de talento para el deporte – ¡genial! Fue muy entretenido. Luego, participé en una clase de chino y aunque la clase misma era divertida, encontré la lengua dificilísima y un poco fea. Después, pasé una hora en el departamento de música tratando de tocar una guitarra con varios otros chicos y logramos tocar una canción bastante bien, en mi opinión. Me sorprendió porque fue bastante fácil y me divertí. Al final del día, asistí a una sesión de yoga y es poco probable que lo haga otra vez. ¡Nunca me he sentido tan incómodo!

How did Roberto feel about these activities? Write the correct letter in each box.

1 volleyball

A	Pleased that he was good at it
B	Disappointed he had no talent
C	Confused as he hadn't played before

☐ (1 mark)

2 Chinese

A	Awful – he didn't enjoy the class
B	Great – he might carry on learning it
C	Fun session but not a nice language

☐ (1 mark)

3 guitar

A	Not great, harder than expected
B	OK, they performed quite well
C	A waste of an hour

☐ (1 mark)

4 yoga

A	Fine, he helped run the session
B	OK, he'll probably have another go
C	He won't be trying it again

☐ (1 mark)

The three key questions in the **skills boosts** will help you infer meaning from what is written in a text.

1 How do I infer positive and negative ideas?

2 How do I infer opinions and justifications?

3 How do I infer meaning by combining information from different parts of a text?

1 How do I infer positive and negative ideas?

Some of the more challenging questions will ask you to deduce positive and negative ideas from quite complex language, without using obvious phrases such as *me gusta* or *fue fantástico*.

① The following adjectives are all taken from the GCSE vocabulary list. Highlight 🖉 the positive adjectives in one colour and the negative ones in a different colour.

afortunado	decepcionante	genial	inseguro	precioso	antipático	avaro
celoso	cobarde	cortés	educado	vago	torpe	asqueroso	nocivo	atento

② Positive and negative ideas can also be inferred from verbs. Complete the table by:

a writing 🖉 P (positive) or N (negative) for each of these Spanish verbs and phrases.

b writing 🖉 the English meaning of each one, looking them up if you do not know them.

Spanish	P/N	English
tener suerte		
disfrutar		
enfadar		
estar harto de		

Spanish	P/N	English
fastidiar		
tener miedo		
sonreírse		
tener ganas		

③ Read the Spanish sentences below.

i Highlight 🖉 the words / phrases that convey a positive or negative idea, using a different colour for each.

ii Then, write 🖉 P (positive), N (negative) or P+N (positive and negative) at the end of each one.

> Remember that *pero* or *aunque* often indicate a contradiction, so it's possible that mixed opinions are being expressed.

> The opinions are mainly conveyed through the verbs and the adjectives, so ensure you focus on these.

a Tenía una manera muy antipática y su actitud me fastidió.

b Es un tipo muy vago pero me hace sonreír.

c Puede ser cortés y atento a veces aunque en esto ha sido muy desconsiderado.

d Vale la pena explorar la ciudad porque tiene muchos rincones preciosos.

e No hemos tenido mucha suerte con el tiempo y estoy harto de tanta lluvia.

f Las vistas eran geniales; en cambio me decepcionó el servicio.

g Me enfada muchísimo tener que pagar estos precios excesivos.

h Disfruté de mi visita enormemente y tengo ganas de volver.

Skills boost

2 · How do I infer opinions and justifications?

Sometimes you will need to deduce an opinion or reaction from a part of the text that does not contain obvious positive or negative vocabulary. In these cases, you need to understand what is being said and use it to arrive at your conclusion.

1 Look at the language used in the descriptions to deduce the emotion of the person involved.

i Highlight ✏ the phrases in the descriptions that provide clues to the emotion.

ii Then draw ✏ an emoji for the emotion expressed. | angry nervous happy / delighted sad |

	Description	Emoji
a	Esta fue la oportunidad que siempre había buscado, fue un sueño convertido en realidad. Tenía ganas de cantar, de correr y de besar a todo el mundo.	
b	Esta fue su primera actuación en público. Patricia tenía la boca seca y las manos temblaban; estaba segura que olvidaría la música o se caería antes de llegar al piano.	
c	Susana salió del salón, cerrando la puerta ruidosamente. Sus padres eran tan antipáticos, prohibiéndola que fuera al concierto con su novio. Quería gritar.	
d	Al leer el mensaje, Elisa estuvo a punto de llorar. Había imaginado un futuro junto con Carlos y ahora, con estas pocas palabras, su futuro entero había desaparecido.	

2 i Read each text and decide if it is positive or negative, writing ✏ P or N in the box.

ii Highlight ✏ the words / phrases that lead you to that conclusion.

iii Look at the words you highlighted. What is the main idea they're expressing? Write ✏ this as the justification for your answers.

> *In the exam, always look at the example to see the type of answer required. Here you can see that the justification is just a summary of the general idea: 'He thinks it's cruel'.*

Example

> No tengo la menor intención de acompañaros. No me apetece la idea de ver el sufrimiento de un animal como un tipo de espectáculo público.

How does Juan feel about the bullfight? | N | Why? *He thinks it's cruel*

a

> No entiendo la atracción de esa fiesta. ¿Por qué malgastar toda esa comida y cubrirte de tomates para limpiar todo una hora después?

How does Ana feel about the Tomatina? | | Why? ....

b

> Esta no es una fiesta a punto de desaparecer. Los hoteles están llenos y cada año vienen más visitantes, de aquí y del resto del mundo.

How does Jorge feel about the future of las Fallas? | | Why? ....

c

> ¿Una merienda en la playa? No sé si has visto el pronóstico pero dicen que habrá viento en la costa con riesgo de chubascos.

How does Andrés feel about a picnic? | | Why? ....

3 **How do I infer meaning by combining information from different parts of a text?**

Sometimes you will have to arrive at an answer by bringing together information from different parts of a text. The 'magazine quiz'-style question is among the more challenging tasks on the Higher Tier paper. The answer requires information from both the quiz question and the circled answer option.

① Look at this first part of a magazine quiz that your friend Elena has done, then answer the question that follows.

> **¿Usas bien tu tiempo libre?**
>
> 1 ¿A qué hora te levantas los fines de semana?
>
>   A El fin de semana está hecho para guardar cama.
>
>   B Cuando mi mamá me llama.
>
>   Ⓒ Temprano, tengo cosas que hacer.

Do you think Elena makes the most of the weekend? Tick ✓ the correct box.

Yes ☐ No ☐

Give a reason for your answer. ✐

② Thinking about spending your time wisely in an exam, write down ✐ which bits of this quiz you actually need to read to answer the question.

③ Look at these three answers to the question in **①** above. The third one is correct because it brings together the information from the quiz question and the circled answer. Why are the first two answers wrong? Write ✐ your explanation beside each answer.

Yes ✓ No ☐ Reason: *She says she has things to do.*

Yes ✓ No ☐ Reason: *She gets up early.*

Yes ✓ No ☐ Reason: *She gets up early to get things done.*

④ Look at this question that a student has answered wrongly about Elena's answer in the questionnaire about her use of time.

> 2 ¿Cuándo haces tus deberes?
>
>   A El día cuando los recibo.
>
>   Ⓑ En el autobús en camino al instituto.
>
>   C Cuando mis padres insisten que los haga.

Do you think Elena has a responsible attitude to her school work?

Yes ✓ No ☐

Give a reason for your answer.

She gets the bus to school

a Why you think the student has arrived at the wrong conclusion? ✐

b Now write ✐ the correct answer to the question.

Yes ☐ No ☐

Give a reason for your answer.

Your turn!

Here is an exam-style question that requires you to put into practice the skills you have worked on, specifically inferring positive and negative opinions, including where someone is expressing mixed feelings.

1 Start by reading through the exam-style question. Then:

Don't forget that opinions can be inferred from verbs and adverbs as well as adjectives.

a underline (A) the parts of the text that contain information about the topics listed in questions **1–4**, using a different pattern for each topic: weather, bonfire, food, fireworks

b within those underlined sections, highlight the words that imply a negative or positive reaction

c circle (A) any connectives that might link similar feelings or imply mixed feelings.

Now use the skills you have developed to tackle this exam-style question.

Exam-style question

5 November

Read Sofía's letter to her family telling them about her experience of Bonfire Night.

No sé cómo logran tener fiestas al aire libre en este país porque anoche hizo un frío intolerable y un viento helado soplaba. A pesar de esto, la familia y yo fuimos en coche a un pub en el campo que tenía un jardín grande para organizar los eventos de la noche. La hoguera era enorme e impresionante y también, afortunadamente, daba bastante calor – lo que apreciábamos. Sobre las siete, se podía ir a comprar comida caliente: hamburguesas, perritos calientes y patatas asadas en el horno. Probé un perrito caliente y lo encontré asqueroso, de muy baja calidad. Sin embargo, la hamburguesa era riquísima y devoré cada bocado. Después empezó el espectáculo de fuegos artificiales. La primera parte fue lenta, incluso aburrida, y me sentí decepcionada, pero al poco rato* mejoró muchísimo y hubo luces y colores por todas partes del cielo.

*al poco rato – soon after

Remember not all adjectives that indicate positive or negative ideas will be straightforward. This word is easy to work out as it's a cognate.

You might not know this word but the phrase following it indicates whether it is positive or negative.

How did Sofía feel about the following?

Write **P** (Positive), **N** (Negative) or **P+N** (Positive and Negative).

1   The weather   (1 mark)

2   The bonfire   (1 mark)

3   The food   (1 mark)

4   The fireworks   (1 mark)

Your turn!

Here is an exam style question that requires you to put into practice the skills that you have worked on, specifically to help you infer meaning, opinions and justifications.

(**1**) Read the exam-style question below.

a First underline (A) the parts of the text that contain information relevant to each question, using a different pattern for each question.

b Next, highlight the positive and negative words in the highlighted sections.

c Then circle any connectives to make sure that you notice whether they affect the meaning.

Now use the skills you have developed to tackle this exam-style question.

Exam-style question

Adventure sports

You read this article about adventure sports in a Spanish newspaper.

> Los deportes de aventura, especialmente los deportes aéreos, implican graves riesgos para los participantes. Cada año hay más aficionados que prueban estos deportes de aventura en España, atraídos por una nueva experiencia y por el reto de enfrentarse al miedo que dan estos deportes.
>
> Casi todos contienen un riesgo considerable. Si no se tienen en cuenta las medidas de seguridad apropiadas, su práctica puede llegar a ser trágica. Hace menos de un mes murió un joven practicando el parapente* en las playas de Benidorm. En doce meses ha habido cuatro accidentes mortales de jóvenes que practicaban este deporte en la zona. "La mayoría de los accidentes se producen por negligencias de jóvenes que no toman en serio el peligro", explica el presidente de la Federación de Deportes Aéreos, Jesús Martínez. "No estamos satisfechos con la situación y estamos intentando regular más estos deportes. Además, queremos cambiar la ley para que no puedan comprar material de vuelo sin el permiso de la Federación."

parapente – paragliding

Write the correct answer in each box.

1 How do young people see adventure sports?

A	Dangerous and expensive
B	A new, if scary, challenge
C	Something that everyone should try

(1 mark)

2 What has happened recently in Benidorm.

A	Benidorm beaches closed after a death
B	Twelve fatalities in extreme sport accidents
C	Four fatal paragliding accidents in a year

(1 mark)

Answer the questions in **English**.

3 Who is to blame for the accidents, according to Jesús Martínez, and why?

.... (1 mark)

4 Is Jesús Martínez happy with the current health and safety precautions? Tick the correct box.

Yes [ ]   No [ ]

Give a reason for your answer.

.... (1 mark)

Review your skills

Check up

Review your responses to the exam-style questions on pages 47 and 48. Tick ✓ the column that shows how well you think you have done each of the following.

	Not quite ✓	Nearly there ✓	Got it! ✓
inferred positive and negative ideas	☐	☐	☐
inferred opinions and justifications	☐	☐	☐
inferred meaning by combining information from different parts of a text	☐	☐	☐

Need more practice?

Go back to pages 42 and 43 and complete ✐ the exam-style questions there. Use the checklist to help you. ✓

Checklist Before I answer the questions, have I...	✓
used my knowledge of adjectives and verbs to identify positive and negative ideas?	
considered any connectives that may help me spot similar or contradicted opinions?	
used all the relevant information in the question and the text to arrive at the correct answer?	

How confident do you feel about each of these **skills**? Colour in ✐ the bars.

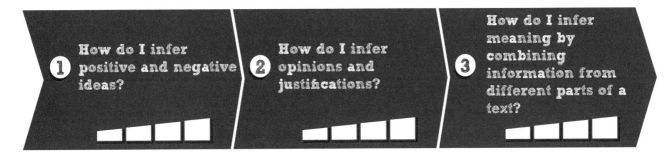

1. How do I infer positive and negative ideas?
2. How do I infer opinions and justifications?
3. How do I infer meaning by combining information from different parts of a text?

(7) Using clues to understand unfamiliar language

This unit will help you use all the available clues to help you deal with vocabulary that you don't know. The skills you will build are to:

- tackle a task that looks very challenging
- identify 'false friends'
- use strategies to understand unfamiliar words.

In the exam you will be asked to do reading tasks similar to the one on the opposite page. This unit will prepare you to cope with complex texts such as extracts from newspapers, magazines and literature.

(1) You can often use clues from elsewhere in the sentence to work out unfamiliar words. Identify which job is mentioned in bold in each sentence below, and write in (✐) the English for that job.

a | Creo que sería muy interesante controlar el dinero y las finanzas de una gran empresa. También ser **contable** sería un trabajo muy responsable.

....

c | Cuando el **cartero** vino a la puerta esta mañana, llevó varias cartas y una tarjeta postal. ¡Esta vez el perro no lo atacó!

....

b | Después de estudiar el derecho en la universidad, un **abogado** ayuda al público con los asuntos legales, desde el divorcio hasta mudarse de casa.

....

d | No quiero ser **granjero** como mi padre: no me interesa la vida rural cuidando a los animales y los campos.

....

Do not answer this exam-style question yet. You will be asked to at the end of the unit.

Exam-style question

The work of a translator

You read this description of the tasks that a translator undertakes.

> Traducir significa, en latín, 'hacer pasar de un lugar a otro', en este caso de un idioma a otro. Esta es la tarea que realiza el traductor, en ámbitos muy distintos, desde una novela policíaca o un poema romántico hasta el manual de instrucciones de una lavadora. También, los traductores trabajan con artículos científicos, documentos legales o subtítulos de películas. Para ello tienes que dominar el texto, pero también el contexto: necesitas entender completamente el asunto de qué se trata. Se requiere un gran dominio de los idiomas, un extenso vocabulario y un amor por la precisión. El traductor trabaja por escrito, armado con un buen diccionario. Pasa muchas horas frente al ordenador, por lo que debe cuidar su postura y proteger la vista.

Answer the questions in **English**.

1 What two literary projects for a translator are mentioned?

....

(1 mark)

2 What might a translator work on for a domestic appliance company?

....

(1 mark)

3 Where might a translator have a role in the world of cinema?

....

(1 mark)

4 As well as fluency in the language, what other two skills are required?

....

(1 mark)

5 What advice is given in the last sentence and why?

....

(1 mark)

The three key questions in the **skills boosts** will help you use clues to understand unfamiliar language.

1 How do I tackle a task that looks very challenging?

2 How do I identify 'false friends'?

3 How do I use strategies to understand unfamiliar words?

1 **How do I tackle a task that looks very challenging?**

Remember: you don't have to understand every word to be able to tackle a comprehension passage. Start by reading the questions, so you can scan the text to find the relevant information. You will see then that some of the words you don't know are not needed anyway!

1 Look at the short texts in Spanish. Highlight 🖉 the parts of the text that you understand and can translate.

A Al rellenar la solicitud, José se preguntó cómo iba a convencer a los directores de que tenía la confianza y la autoridad de ser el jefe de una oficina entera.

C El primer día le gastaron bromas, le mandaron a buscar herramientas inexistentes y le pusieron sal en el café. Carlos pensó que aceptar el trabajo había sido un gran error.

B El vestíbulo era amplio e imponente, desconcertando a Sara con su impresión de grandeza. Pero Sara sabía que estaba bien vestida, bien preparada y puntual.

D 'Habrás notado la escasez de estudiantes hoy' interrumpió la directora. 'Es que están de huelga. Pero no te preocupes, Laura, estarán aquí cuando empieces el mes que viene'.

2 Now look at the questions below, relating to texts **A–D**.

i Highlight 🖉 the key words in the questions that will help you find the answer in the text.

ii Under each question, note down 🖉 in English what the question is asking.

a ¿Qué trabajo quería hacer José?

....

b ¿Cómo sabemos que Sara se había organizado bien para la entrevista?

....

c ¿Cuál fue la conclusión de Carlos al final de su primer día?

....

d ¿Cuándo empieza Laura su nuevo trabajo como profesora?

....

3 Now go back to the texts in **1** and underline Ⓐ the information needed to answer the questions in **2**.

When answering a question, look for the information you need in a part of the text where the vocabulary is more accessible and where you have already highlighted words you know.

4 Now answer 🖉 the questions from **2** in **Spanish**.

a ....

b ....

c ....

d ....

Remember you can lift answers in Spanish directly from the text, so you won't need to change anything as long as you find the right section.

2 How do I identify 'false friends'?

'False friends' are Spanish words that look very similar to English words, but actually mean something different. Learning the most common ones and being able to spot where an English translation sounds odd will help ensure they don't catch you out.

(1) The table below contains some common 'false friends'. To help you learn them:

Create a special section in your vocabulary book to note down 'false friends'.

a first, next to each Spanish word, write down ✎ the English word it looks like

b next, write down ✎ what each word really means, looking up any you don't know

c in the far-right column, note down ✎ a phrase to help you remember the real meaning.

Spanish	Looks like	Really means	Memorable phrase
largo	large	long	un lago largo (a long lake)
sano			
campo			
lectura			
sensible			
éxito			
arena			
actual			

(2) You can often spot if you have wrongly translated a 'false friend' because it will not sound right or make sense in the context. Look at the translations of the Spanish sentences below.

i Cross out ~~cat~~ the word that sounds odd.

ii Then write ✎ a better translation of the word in the space provided.

a | El nombre de la empresa es Coltran. | *The number of the company is Coltran.* ....

b | Voy a la librería para comprar una novela. | *I'm going to the library to buy a novel.* ....

c | El conductor del taxi causó el accidente. | *The taxi conductor caused the accident.* ....

d | La carpeta contiene mis notas de la universidad. | *The carpet contains my university notes.*

....

e | ¡Qué risa! Es un chiste muy gracioso. | *How funny! It's a very gracious joke.* ....

(3) The text below contains eight 'false friends'.

a Underline Ⓐ each 'false friend'.

b On paper, write down ✎ each word, its 'false friend' meaning and its real meaning.

> En ese tiempo, en mi trabajo en la agencia de detectives, sentía una profunda decepción con el empleo. Cada día en la oficina era lo mismo y nada nuevo sucedía. Había decidido que ya no lo soportaba cuando, una mañana, el jefe me llamó a su despacho. "Últimamente pareces un poco distraída, Cristina", dijo "y creo que es porque el trabajo no te ofrece mucho desafío. Tienes demasiado talento para quedarte como secretaria y quiero ofrecerte la oportunidad de hacerte detective. Asistirás a la universidad un día a la semana para estudiar psicología y realizarás varios proyectos independientes. La formación durará un año pero, después, tienes que recordar que tu salario subirá."

3 How do I use strategies to understand unfamiliar words?

Sometimes, working out unknown words is like being a detective. You have to use the various clues to arrive at the most logical conclusion.

① Read this extract from *Donde aprenden a volar las gaviotas* by Ana Alcolea, where Arturo found out how he was to spend the summer.

> (...) Me empaquetaron rumbo a Noruega con una familia a la que no conocía. El padre era colega del mío en una Universidad y experto en algún rey islandés de las sagas, que son esos poemas épicos nórdicos que están llenos de sangre*, batallas y cabezas cortadas. La madre trabajaba en una fábrica de chocolates. Tenían un hijo que, por supuesto, se llamaba Erik y era rubio como la cerveza.

*sangre – blood

In the first sentence, you may not know the words *empaquetaron*, *rumbo*, and *Noruega*.

a Start by looking at *empaquetaron*. Circle Ⓐ the correct answers.

 i   What tense is it in?   present / future / preterite

 ii Looking at the verb's ending, who is doing the action?   I / we / they

 iii What does the noun *paquete* mean?   page / parcel / park

 iv Who is the object in *me empaquetaron*?   them / him / me

b Now look at *Noruega* and answer ✎ the following questions.

 i   Why might it have a capital letter? ....

 ii It is preceded by *a*. What does this mean? ....

 iii Say 'Noruega' out loud. Does it sound like somewhere you have heard of? ....

c Try translating *me empaquetaron rumbo a Noruega* and write ✎ it below. You will find you don't need to know *rumbo* for the sentence to make sense.

....

② The second sentence contains several cognates or near-cognates (such as *colega*, meaning 'colleague'). Write down ✎ each one with its English translation.

Example *Universidad – university*

....

....

③ See how the word *islandés* in the second sentence is similar to *irlandés*. Note down ✎:

a what type of word it is likely to be ....

b what you think it might mean. ....

④ On paper, answer ✎ the following questions:

a What were Arturo's parents planning to do with him that summer?

c How does he describe 'sagas'?

b What was the father of the family an expert in?

d What was the mother's job?

Your turn!

Here is an exam-style question that will help you to practise tackling challenging texts, specifically by making the most of clues and by being wary of 'false friends'. 🖉

Exam-style question

Daniel joins the Sempere family business

Read this extract adapted from *La sombra del viento*, a novel by Carlos Ruiz Zafón, and answer the questions which follow in **English**.

> Cuando no estaba en el colegio o con Clara, todo mi tiempo lo dedicaba a ayudar a mi padre en la librería. Ordenando el almacén de la trastienda (…) o atendiendo a los clientes habituales. Mi padre se quejaba de que no ponía la cabeza ni el corazón en el trabajo. Yo, a mi vez, replicaba que me pasaba la vida entera allí y que no entendía de qué tenía que quejarse.
>
> Las cosas en la librería se estaban animando y mi padre y yo teníamos más trabajo del que podíamos quitarnos de encima. "A este paso vamos a tener que coger a otra persona para que nos ayude en la búsqueda de los pedidos*" comentaba mi padre. "Lo que nos haría falta sería alguien muy especial, medio detective, medio poeta, que cobre barato y al que no le asusten de las misiones imposibles." "Creo que tengo al candidato adecuado" dije.

*un pedido – an order   *asustar – to frighten

Remember to be wary of 'false friends'. Daniel works in *una librería*. What is it?

Use linguistic detective tactics to work out words like *trastienda*: 'tras' is part of *detrás* (behind), and *tienda* means 'shop'.

1   What was Daniel's role in the business?

....

(1 mark)

2   Was Daniel's father happy with the way his son worked? Yes ☐ No ☐
Give a reason for your answer.

....

(1 mark)

3   How do we know the Sempere family business was doing well?

....

(1 mark)

4   What skills is Sr Sempere looking for in a potential new employee?

....

(1 mark)

5   What other factors would make a candidate very employable, according to Sr Sempere?

....

(1 mark)

Keep your eyes open for useful cognates such as: *dedicar, atender, cliente, comentar, especial, detective*. What English words do they look like?

Your turn!

Here is an exam-style question that requires you to put into practice the skills that you have worked on, specifically to help you tackle texts such as literary extracts. 🖉

Exam-style question

The interview

Read this extract adapted from *La mujer habitada*, a novel by Gioconda Belli.

> El día que llegó a la entrevista de trabajo, Lavinia se paró en cada piso. Eran todos parecidos. Grandes puertas de madera y los letreros en caracteres dorados. Empujó las puertas de madera de la firma "Arquitectos Asociados S.A." y se encontró en el vestíbulo sobrio y moderno, frente a la secretaria modosa de ojos verdes que le pidió sentarse. El señor Solera la recibiría en un momento. Tomó una revista y encendió un cigarrillo.

Write the correct letter in each box.

1 Lavinia took the lift, which…

A	went to the top floor.
B	stopped on every level.
C	took her down from her flat.

(1 mark)

2 The building was full of offices with…

A	wooden doors and plaques in gold.
B	glass windows and busy employees.
C	bright lights and modern fittings.

(1 mark)

3 She went into the reception…

A	and was invited to take a seat.
B	but the secretary was on the phone.
C	noticing the antique furnishings.

(1 mark)

4 The secretary told her that the boss…

A	was out at the moment.
B	would be a while, but she could wait.
C	would be with her shortly.

(1 mark)

Take heart from the words that you *do* know. Don't be put off by unknown vocabulary; you won't need to know it all!

Read the questions first and use highlighters to flag up the sections of the text you are going to need. You may not need to understand the sections containing complex vocabulary.

Review your skills

Check up

Review your responses to the exam-style questions on pages 55 and 56. Tick ⊘ the column that shows how well you think you have done each of the following.

	Not quite ⊘	Nearly there ⊘	Got it! ⊘
tackled a task that looked very challenging	☐	☐	☐
identified 'false friends'	☐	☐	☐
used strategies to understand unfamiliar words	☐	☐	☐

Need more practice?

Go back to page 51 and complete ✎ the exam-style question there. Use the checklist to help you. ⊘

Checklist Before I answer the questions, have I...	⊘
read the questions and scanned the texts so that I focus only on the sections that will be needed?	
considered any 'false friends' that might mislead my understanding of the text?	
used the clues within unknown words to help me work out their root and meaning?	

How confident do you feel about each of these **skills**? Colour in ✎ the bars.

1. How do I tackle a task that looks very challenging?

2. How do I identify 'false friends'?

3. How do I use strategies to understand unfamiliar words?

⑧ Translating accurately into English

This unit will help you overcome the challenges faced when translating from Spanish into English.

The skills you will build are to:

- ensure that you have covered all key elements
- work out unknown vocabulary
- avoid sounding stilted and unnatural.

In the exam you will be asked to do a translation task similar to the ones on these two pages.

Do not answer the exam-style question yet. You will be asked to at the end of the unit.

Exam-style question

You see this news item in an online magazine. Translate it into **English** for your family.

> A pesar del mal tiempo, Ana está en la playa, ayudando a quitar la basura del mar y de la arena. "Hemos visto un programa sobre los efectos del plástico en los peces y los animales del océano. Estas bolsas y botellas harán daño a la vida marina y vamos a limpiar esta parte de la costa."

(9 marks)

Make sure you learn this conjunction. It looks like an infinitive (*pesar* – to weigh), but the phrase *a pesar de* means 'in spite of'.

If you don't know this word, can you think of any word it looks similar to?

Think of a few different English synonyms for this, then pick the one that sounds most natural as part of the whole sentence. If you are unsure, use a dictionary and look at the various options given there.

Often a translation can sound unnatural because a preposition has been mistranslated. For example, *un libro por Isabel Allende* is not a book *for* Isabel Allende, but a book *by* Isabel Allende.

(1) For each Spanish preposition listed below, find the English equivalent in the word box. Write 🖉 the English next to the Spanish.

between / among	for / through / by	from / since
in order to / for	in / on of / from	on / about
~~to / at~~ with	without	

Most Spanish prepositions have more than one meaning in English. It is important to learn these and consider them when you are translating. For example, *entre tú y yo* sounds odd as 'among you and I', but perfectly natural as 'between you and me'.

Example a: *to / at* ....

con: ....   en: ....   por: ....

de: ....   entre: ....   sin: ....

desde: ....   para: ....   sobre: ....

Do not answer the exam-style question yet. You will be asked to at the end of the unit.

Exam-style question

Your friend has picked up this leaflet and wants to know what it says.
Translate it into **English** for your friend.

> ¿Sufres el sobrepeso? ¿Quieres perder unos kilos? Es mucho más fácil lograr este propósito si te haces miembro de un club. Aquí ofrecemos consejo e ideas para comidas que son ricas pero bajas en calorías. Con nuestro apoyo tendrás un cuerpo delgado y sano. 'Yo asistí al club y perdí once kilos en tres semanas', dice Luisa.

Think carefully about how you'll translate the prepositions.

(9 marks)

....
....
....
....
....
....
....
....
....
....

The three key questions in the **skills boosts** will help you overcome the challenges you face when translating from Spanish into English.

 1 How do I ensure that I have included all key elements?

 2 How do I work out unknown vocabulary?

 3 How do I avoid sounding stilted and unnatural?

1 **How do I ensure that I have included all key elements?**

In the translation task, marks are awarded for conveying each key idea of the text. It's important not to miss an element out, or you will lose the mark for that section.

When you are proofreading, trace the line of the Spanish text with your finger while your eye moves over the translation.

① Read the translations by students of sentences **a–d** below. A teacher has indicated where each student has missed something out. Read both the Spanish and the English carefully and write in ✎ the missing word(s) next to the omission mark (^).

Ensure you pay attention to seemingly unimportant small words, like *casi*, *más* and *todas*.

a Hay que apagar todas las luces al final del día.

We must turn off ^ .... the lights at the end of the day.

b Tuvieron que evacuar a más de mil personas.

They had to evacuate ^ .... a thousand people.

c Los gamberros ya no hacen daño al parque.

The hooligans don't damage the park ^ ....

d Hay casi quinientos 'sin techo' en la ciudad.

There are ^ .... five hundred homeless people in the town.

② Now it's your turn to spot what has been missed out. Read these sentences and their translations, ticking ✓ each Spanish word when you are sure it has been dealt with. Then write in ✎ the omission mark at the correct point in the sentence, and write ✎ the missing word(s) in the space provided.

a Hay mucho tráfico y, por eso, la contaminación es nociva.

There is a lot of traffic and the pollution is harmful. ....

Break up the Spanish into phrases and look at each one in turn to make sure that the translation deals with all the vocabulary.

b Este animal es otra especie en peligro de extinción.

This animal is a species in danger of extinction. ....

c El petrolero se hundió a eso de las tres de la mañana.

The oil tanker sank at three in the morning. ....

d Todavía queda mucho por hacer para proteger la selva.

There is a lot to be done in order to protect the rainforest. ....

③ i Read the sentences and highlight ✎ any small but important words you think you might miss.

ii Then, on paper, translate ✎ the sentences into English.

a Esta ley no resolverá el problema de los envases tampoco.

b La drogadicción es aun peor entre los 'sin techo'.

c El efecto invernadero es tal vez el tema más urgente.

d Ya hemos visto varios accidentes este año.

e Me preocupa bastante la falta de igualdad en el trabajo.

Always proofread your work. Read the English to ensure it sounds natural and makes sense, but also read the Spanish to check that you haven't missed anything out.

② How do I work out unknown vocabulary?

If you don't know a word, have an educated guess rather than leave it out. If you use the context and other clues, your linguistic common sense will help lead you to the right translation.

① Look at the example sentence below. You might not know the word *estaciones*, but by translating the rest of the sentence you can have a sensible guess at what it might mean.

> Remember, when dealing with unfamiliar words: try breaking them down into smaller parts to see if you recognise the root of a word; consider whether it's related to a similar word that you do know; use the context.

i Translate 🖉 the sentences below, circling Ⓐ the correct translation for each underlined word from the three options.

ii Now highlight 🖉 the words in each Spanish sentence that helped you decide.

iii Note down 🖉 how these words gave you clues.

Example   De las cuatro <u>estaciones</u> del año, el verano es cuando hay más contaminación.

Translation: *Of the four seasons in a year, summer is when there is more pollution*

Notes: *cuatro… del año means four… in a year; verano means summer, so estación = season*

a Para tener un trabajo en la piscina, necesito un certificado de <u>primeros auxilios</u>.

   Options: food hygiene / first-aid / grade one

   Translation: ....

   Notes: ....

b Lo bueno es que dicen que hay menos <u>agujeros</u> en la capa de ozono.

   Options: pollution / problems / holes

   Translation: ....

   Notes: ....

c En algunos países los <u>deshechos</u> de las fábricas todavía entran en los ríos.

   Options: waste / chimneys / workers

   Translation: ....

   Notes: ....

② Now, on paper, translate 🖉 the Spanish sentences, using the skills you have developed to work out the underlined word. As in ①, note down 🖉 what clues you used to work it out.

a Después del escape de combustible del petrolero, la <u>marea negra</u> está afectando los animales y pájaros de la costa.

b Queremos llevar <u>mantas</u> de lana a los 'sin techo': serán mejores que los periódicos viejos que usan.

c Con la falta de ejercicio y todos los restaurantes de comida rápida, el <u>sobrepeso</u> es un problema grave en nuestra sociedad.

d Sin lluvia significativa en dos años, el país sufre la peor <u>sequía</u> en cincuenta años.

③ On paper, translate 🖉 this passage into English.

> Ayer tuvimos una clase sobre los peligros del tabaquismo. El profesor explicó los efectos médicos muy sencillamente para que fuera fácil de entender. Además, nos advirtió de las otras desventajas como el olor asqueroso y el color amarillento de los dientes. Dejé la clase completamente convencida de que no iba a fumar jamás en la vida.

3 How do I avoid sounding stilted and unnatural?

The art of translation is to stay as close as possible to the meaning of the original text and, at the same time, produce language that sounds totally natural. After completing a translation, read it again a short while later. Often you can see expressions that you need to alter because they sound odd or stilted.

① Look in the word box to find the correct English translation of the Spanish phrases in the table. Write ✐ the English next to its Spanish equivalent. These are either idioms or expressions that are not translated word-for-word. You will need to know them.

| tonight | to have a good time | everywhere | to agree to |

Spanish	English
por todas partes	
esta noche	
quedar en	
pasarlo bien	

② Now look at the following translations attempted by a student, featuring the expressions from ①.

i First underline Ⓐ the stilted and unnatural section of each translation.

ii Then rewrite ✐ the mistranslated section correctly.

a Lo pasé muy bien trabajando en la tienda solidaria.

I spent it very well working in the charity shop. ....

b Vamos a limpiar la playa: hay basura por todas partes.

We're going to clean up the beach; there is rubbish in all parts. ....

c Quedaron en recaudar fondos para los 'sin techo'.

They stayed in to collect funds for the homeless. ....

d Dicen que esta noche hay una posibilidad de inundaciones.

They say that this night there is a chance of floods. ....

③ The use of the definite article is different in Spanish and English. When generalising, the definite articles *el, la, los, las* are used in Spanish, but 'the' is left out in English. Cross out ⊘ the articles that should be omitted in the English translations.

a La drogadicción es un problema grave en la sociedad.

The drug addiction is a serious problem in the society.

b Las mujeres sufren la discriminación en el mundo laboral.

The women suffer the discrimination in the world of work.

> Be careful of word order here; how will you deal with *de*? For example, *Soy estudiante de derecho* would be translated as 'I'm a law student'.

c En los próximos cincuenta años tenemos que resolver el problema del calentamiento global.

In the next fifty years we have to solve the problem of the global warming.

④ Now, on paper, translate ✐ the following sentences into English. Once you have finished, read through your answers using the checklist on page 63.

a Por un lado, las temperaturas son menos extremas pero, por otro lado, las inundaciones son más frecuentes.

b Tengo diecisiete años. Mi cumpleaños fue hace dos semanas.

c No entiendo esta palabra. ¿Qué quiere decir?

d Es profesora de geografía en el instituto de mi hermana.

Your turn!

Here is an exam-style question that requires you to put into practice the skills you have worked on, specifically tackling unknown vocabulary and translating all the key elements in a natural-sounding way.

Exam-style question

Your Spanish friend has sent you this email. Translate it into **English** for your family.

Cada año nuestro instituto organiza una semana de actividades con fines benéficos y los estudiantes realizan trabajo voluntario. El octubre pasado ayudé en una residencia para ancianos y toqué el piano en el salón de los residentes. La semana que viene estaré en la ciudad preparando sopa caliente para los 'sin techo'.

(9 marks)

Look out for phrases that need extra thought as they will sound very stilted if translated literally.

Realizar is a famous 'false friend'. Can you work out what it means from its context?

Think carefully about whether you need to translate the article here.

Remember to tick off the words in Spanish as you deal with them to ensure you leave nothing out.

Checklist	⊘
Once you've written the translations, check to see whether you've included any articles that are not needed in English.	
Re-read the English without looking at the Spanish. Underline any parts that don't sound natural.	
Read the Spanish again to make sure you've understood the gist, then revise your English sentence if necessary to make it more idiomatic.	

Your turn!

Here is an exam style question that requires you to put into practice the skills that you have worked on, to help you tackle all aspects of the translation exercise. 🖉

Exam-style question

Your Spanish friend has sent you this text message. Translate it into **English** for your family.

> Anoche tuvimos una tormenta en el pueblo con lluvias intensas durante tres horas. Esta mañana inundaciones siguen afectando el centro y muchas casas están bajo agua. Hay basura por todas partes y mis amigos y yo hemos quedado en participar en la operación de limpieza. ¡El calentamiento global tiene efectos inesperados!

(9 marks)

Remember that you met *por todas partes* and *quedar en* earlier in the unit. Can you remember what they mean?

When translating *el calentamiento global*, think carefully about the Spanish/English difference in the use of the article.

Use your communication strategies to work out *inesperado*. What can *esperar* mean? What does the prefix *in-* do to the meaning of a word?

Review your skills

Check up

Review your responses to the exam-style questions on pages 63 and 64. Tick ✓ the column that shows how well you think you have done each of the following.

	Not quite ✓	Nearly there ✓	Got it! ✓
ensured that I have covered all key elements	☐	☐	☐
worked out unknown vocabulary	☐	☐	☐
avoided sounding stilted and unnatural	☐	☐	☐

Need more practice?

Go back to pages 58 and 59 and complete ✎ the exam-style questions there. Use the checklist to help you. ✓

Checklist Before I answer the questions, have I...	✓
re-read the original text and my translation to check that I have dealt with all the key elements?	
used the make-up of the word and its context to work out any unknown vocabulary?	
considered idiomatic expressions and the use of the article to avoid sounding stilted and unnatural?	

How confident do you feel about each of these **skills**? Colour in ✎ the bars.

1 How do I ensure that I have covered all key elements?	2 How do I work out unknown vocabulary?	3 How do I avoid sounding stilted and unnatural?
☐☐☐☐	☐☐☐☐	☐☐☐☐

More practice questions

Exam-style question

Teachers

You read this post by Inés on a Spanish online forum, where students talk about what makes the ideal teacher.

Me acuerdo de mi profesora de química que era una señora muy inteligente y profesional. Desde el principio, nos trataba como individuos y siempre hacía un esfuerzo por conocernos. Me gustó tanto porque se interesaba por nosotros y usaba su conocimiento de nuestra personalidad y habilidades para ayudarnos cuando teníamos problemas con la ciencia. Todos la respetábamos y si alguna vez tenía por qué reñirnos*, sentíamos mucha vergüenza porque sabíamos que la habíamos decepcionado. Al contrario, la profesora de biología era una histérica y tengo que confesar que la tratábamos muy mal, comportándonos como niños tontos y traviesos en su clase. ¡Cómo debe habernos odiado!

Inés

reñir – to quarrel / tell off

Answer the questions in **English**.

Example How did the Chemistry teacher treat her pupils from the start?

She treated them like individuals and always tried to get to know them

1 How did the Chemistry teacher's interest in her students enable her to help them better?

....

....

(1 mark)

2 How did students feel when the Chemistry teacher told them off? Why did they feel like this?

....

....

(1 mark)

3 In what way did Inés and her friends treat the Biology teacher badly?

....

....

(1 mark)

4 What does Inés assume about her Biology teacher?

....

....

(1 mark)

Jorge's holiday journey

You pick up the book your Spanish friend is reading and look at the first few lines.

> El año pasado reservé alojamiento en un albergue juvenil en Galicia y me despedí de mis padres en el andén antes de coger el tren al norte. Tuve que hacer transbordo una vez en Madrid pero no tenía mucho equipaje así que todo resultó fácil. El ferrocarril aquí en España funciona bastante bien y el tren llegó sin retraso, a pesar de las muchas paradas que hizo. Al llegar al albergue, decidí pagar un poco más para tener la media pensión. Me pareció más conveniente.

Write the correct letter in each box.

1   What did Jorge do before his journey?

A	Book a hotel
B	Reserve his seat
C	Say goodbye to his parents

(1 mark)

2   Why was the train journey straightforward?

A	He was travelling light.
B	He didn't have to change.
C	It was a high-speed city train.

(1 mark)

3   What do we learn about his arrival?

A	He arrived on time.
B	It was close to the bus stop.
C	The train was briefly delayed.

(1 mark)

4   What did he do when he got to the place he was staying?

A	Paid more to have a better room
B	Opted to go half-board
C	Found a more convenient hostel

(1 mark)

A Mexican soap opera

You read this summary of last week's programme.

Se acabó la gran amistad entre los gemelos, Ricardo y Roberto, cuando se pelearon después de que Ricardo se disfrazó como su hermano para salir con su chica, la hermosa Anita. Ella solo descubrió la verdad al final de la tarde y ahora no sabe cuál de ellos prefiere.

Una hora antes de casarse, Verónica se creía la mujer más feliz del mundo pero una hora después de la boda, su nuevo marido, Jaime, confesó que ya no la quería. Dijo lo sentía mucho pero se marchaba y ella no lo vería nunca más.

Pedro reveló a Lucía que había mentido cuando le dijo que era su padre verdadero y que este era, en efecto, un famoso cantante que no quería asumir las responsabilidades de paternidad. Lucía hizo la decisión de abandonar la casa familiar para ir en busca de su padre para enfrentarle con la verdad de que era su hija.

1 Which **two** statements are true about last week's episode?

Write the correct letters in the boxes.

A	The twins became great friends.
B	A love triangle caused a row.
C	Verónica was jilted just before her wedding.
D	Jaime's marriage came to a sudden end.
E	Pedro confessed to being Lucía's real father.

(2 marks)

2 What did Lucía decide to do? Mention **two** things.

Answer in **English**.

....

....

(2 marks)

Exam-style question

Cómo animar a los jóvenes a hacer deporte

Ves este consejo a los padres en una página web española.

- Hay que dar al adolescente información sobre los beneficios de practicar un deporte. Es muy saludable y les ayudará a hacer más amigos. Además, aporta ventajas que siguen teniendo impacto durante toda la vida.

- Elegir un deporte apropiado para la personalidad del joven. En esto los padres pueden ayudar mucho porque conocen como nadie el carácter y las habilidades de sus hijos y pueden ayudarlos a adquirir la información que necesitan. No obstante*, tiene que ser el adolescente mismo el que tome la decisión.

- Hace falta proveerle del equipo que necesita y facilitarle el transporte. Aunque eso sea un esfuerzo para los padres, vale la pena ya que les dará tiempo para pasar con su hijo adolescente y asegurará que este sepa que tiene su apoyo.

- Ofrecerle un modelo a imitar. Los otros miembros de la familia deben ponerse a practicar algún deporte porque, si no, el adolescente se dará cuenta de la falsedad de su consejo.

*no obstante – however / nonetheless

Contesta las preguntas en **español**.

1 ¿Cuáles son los beneficios del deporte? Menciona **dos** cosas.

....

....

(2 marks)

2 ¿Por qué los padres podrían ayudar a sus hijos a escoger un deporte adecuado?

....

(1 mark)

3 ¿Cuáles son las dos cosas que deben proveer los padres?

....

(1 mark)

4 ¿Qué tienen que hacer los otros miembros de la familia para animar al adolescente?

....

(1 mark)

Arturo arrives in Trondheim

Read this extract from *Donde aprenden a volar las gaviotas*, by Ana Alcolea.

Un tren y tres aviones tuve que coger desde Zaragoza hasta Trondheim, que está en el centro de Noruega y es la tercera ciudad del país. Llegué después de pasear todo el día entre nubes y aeropuertos. Me esperaba toda la familia: el padre, que se llamaba Ivar; Inger, la madre, de larga melena rubia, que parecía sacada de un cómic; y Erik, el hijo, que me llevó las maletas hasta el coche. La primera impresión que tuve de Noruega fue que a finales de junio hacía frío, y la segunda que había mucha luz: a pesar de haber aterrizado a las once y media de la noche, los rayos del sol aún se veían sobre el fiordo.

Write the correct letter in each box.

1   How is Trondheim described?

A	An important city in mid-Norway
B	A short journey from Zaragoza
C	A city with an airport and train station

(1 mark)

2   How is Inger described?

A	As a big woman
B	Like a character from fiction
C	Very tall and fair

(1 mark)

3   What do we learn about his arrival?

A	It was a cold morning.
B	It felt like summer.
C	He landed late at night.

(1 mark)

4   What did Arturo notice second?

A	Sunrise over the fjords
B	That it was still light
C	That he was feeling frightened

(1 mark)

Opinions about tattoos

You read these opinions about tattoos on the forum of a Spanish website.

Los tatuajes* son populares hoy día: el 36% de los jóvenes de entre 18 y 35 años tienen al menos uno. ¿Qué piensas? ¿Te gustan los tatuajes?	
Anselmo	Sí, me gustan mucho. Prefiero los tatuajes pequeños porque creo que son bonitos e interesantes. Los mejores son una verdadera obra de arte. Si cambias de opinión más tarde en la vida es posible quitarlo.
Eva	A mí me parecen un poco sucios y pienso que es un acto demasiado permanente. Estoy segura que muchas personas lamentan tener el tatuaje cuando sean mayores.
Lorenzo	Creo que pueden ser peligrosos porque pueden causar infecciones de la piel. Es muy importante hacer el tatuaje en un sitio oficial porque es fundamental que el proceso sea limpio y sano. Ya que el proceso implica el contacto con la sangre podría haber el peligro de contraer enfermedades como el sida.

*tatuajes – tattoos

Answer the questions in **English**.

1 How does Anselmo describe the best tattoos?

....

(1 mark)

2 Do you think Anselmo would regret having a tattoo?

Yes ☐ No ☐

Give a reason for your answer.

....

(1 mark)

3 Why would Eva not have a tattoo? Give **two** reasons.

....

....

(2 marks)

4 Why does Lorenzo fear that having a tattoo is dangerous? Give **two** reasons.

....

....

(2 marks)

The school system

You read this comparison between the education systems in Spain and England.

> Los institutos españoles son parecidos a los ingleses: son mixtos y los alumnos estudian una amplia gama de asignaturas. No suelen llevar uniforme en los institutos públicos, sólo en los privados.
>
> No tienen centros separados para hacer el bachillerato como en algunas partes de Inglaterra y cuando tienen diecisiete o dieciocho años todavía hacen unas nueve o diez asignaturas. Los estudiantes ingleses sólo estudian tres o cuatro.
>
> Para ir a la universidad los alumnos españoles tienen que hacer los exámenes de selectividad que es un tipo de prueba de acceso. Los hacen en la universidad más cercana y duran unos tres días.

1   Which **two** statements are true?

Write the correct letters in the boxes.

A	Many Spanish schools are single-sex schools.
B	Only a limited range of subjects is available in Spain.
C	State school pupils don't usually wear school uniform in Spain.
D	In Spain, sixth form colleges offer the equivalent of A-level courses.
E	Spanish students do up to ten subjects at age 18.

☐ ☐   (2 marks)

2   What **two** things do we learn about the university entrance exams?
Answer in **English**.

1   ....

2   ....

(2 marks)

Problemas de vacaciones

Ves estos comentarios en un foro sobre las vacaciones desastrosas.

A	Tengo una alergia a los mariscos y pensé que iba a morirme después de comer paella.
B	La policía me aconsejó guardar mis documentos importantes en el hotel en el futuro.
C	Tuve que lavar toda la ropa y no fue posible quitar las manchas rojas de mi camiseta blanca.
D	La maleta no llegó hasta tres días después y tuve que ponerme la ropa de mi amiga.
E	Me rompí la pierna el primer día en la sierra y no pude participar el resto de la semana.
F	El volumen de las risas y los gritos de la tienda de al lado nos impidió dormir la semana entera.
G	La fiesta es tan popular que no hay sitio en ningún hotel ni hostal. No podemos quedar.

Escribe la letra correcta en cada casilla.

1   Una botella de vino se rompió en mi maleta.   (1 mark)

2   El ruido de los vecinos arruinó las vacaciones.   (1 mark)

3   Perdí mi pasaporte.   (1 mark)

4   Un accidente puso fin a mis vacaciones de esquí.   (1 mark)

5   Me sentí muy enfermo.   (1 mark)

Exam-style question

Your Spanish friend has sent you an email. Translate his email into **English** for your family.

Mi hermano mayor, Santi, tiene una entrevista el jueves y está muy nervioso. Hay mucho paro en la ciudad y hay pocos trabajos bien pagados. Santi va a investigar la empresa para que pueda hacer preguntas inteligentes al jefe. Ya se ha comprado un traje nuevo y planeado el viaje.

(9 marks)

Answers

Unit 1

Page 2

 ①

localizado en	situado en
de invierno	invernal
tiene	cuenta con
vista	panorama
situación	localidad
centro histórico	casco antiguo
está muy cerca de	está a cinco minutos de
un sitio relajado	un refugio tranquilo
todo el día	desde la mañana a la noche
las zonas más visitadas	los destinos más turísticos

② ⓐ and ⓑ

2 Quiero unos días en un <u>paisaje verde</u>, disfrutando unos <u>pasatiempos rurales.</u> = green scenery, rural pastimes

3 Necesitamos <u>descansar</u> y que <u>alguien más cuide a los niños</u> un rato. = rest, someone else looking after the children

4 Me gustaría una semana <u>en la costa</u> pero <u>sin miles de veraneantes.</u> = on the coast, without thousands of holidaymakers

5 Siempre me ha interesado <u>el alpinismo</u> y quiero <u>aprender con un instructor.</u> = mountain climbing, learn from an instructor

Page 3

③ A: Situado en la Sierra Nevada, el Hotel Siroco cuenta con los panoramas más exquisitos y los <u>monitores te ayudarán</u> con <u>cualquier deporte invernal que te interese</u> probar.

D: El Gran Hotel Santiago ofrece un <u>nivel de calidad sin precedentes.</u> <u>Cocina de cinco estrellas</u> cada día, peluquería en la planta baja y gimnasio de uso gratuito.

E: Casa El Palomar te ofrece <u>todas las delicias del campo</u>: productos regionales como el queso y el jamón, <u>actividades relajantes como la equitación y la pesca.</u>

F: Si buscas sol y <u>playa</u> pero prefieres <u>evitar las grandes multitudes</u> de los destinos más turísticos, escoge el Hostal Nerina – un secreto bien guardado.

G: Para que <u>los padres podáis relajaros</u> como merecéis, el Hotel Gaviota cuenta con <u>actividades para los pequeños</u> desde la mañana a la noche. ¡Aprovechadlo!

Page 4

① ⓐ

Piso	N	estupendo	A	tormenta	N
Opinar	V	guapo	A	seleccionar	V
Lluvia	N	hogar	N	creer	V

bello	A	apartamento	N	escoger	V
genial	A	elegir	V	hermoso	A
pensar	V	nieve	N	fenomenal	A

ⓑ opinar – looks like opinion, is a verb = 'to be of the opinion'

estupendo – near-cognate = stupendous, marvellous

elegir – similar to 'elect' = to choose

ⓒ Good looking: guapo, bello, hermoso

To think: pensar, creer, opinar

Place to live: apartamento, piso, hogar

Weather: lluvia, nieve, tormenta

Great: fenomenal, genial, estupendo

To choose: seleccionar, escoger, elegir

② ⓐ veranear (V), a orillas del (AP), alojamiento (N), junto a (AP), bañándonos (V), nos retiramos (V), a la sombra (AP), almorzar (V), gazpacho (N)

ⓑ cada agosto – every August; costa – coast; could refer to a summer holiday

nos gusta estar – we like to be; mar – sea; reservamos – we book; la playa – the beach; could refer to somewhere to stay by the sea

pasamos las mañanas – we spend the mornings; en el mediterráneo – in the Mediterranean; could refer to swimming in the sea

Durante las horas de más calor – during the hottest times; unos platos típicos – typical dishes; o mariscos – or seafood; could refer to a type of food

ⓒ veranear – pasar el verano, a orillas del – al lado del, alojamiento – habitaciones, junto a – cerca de, bañándonos – nadando, nos retiramos – nos sentamos, a la sombra – fuera del sol, almorzar – comer, gazpacho – sopa fría

Page 5

① A camión – lorry, averiado – broken down, cruce – crossroads, rueda – wheel

B broncearse – to get a tan, insolación – sunstroke, sombrilla – sunshade

C decepcionado – disappointed, aduana – customs, quejarse – to complain, detener – to stop

D abanico – fan, deseo – wish, castellano – Castilian Spanish

② ⓐ d ⓑ a ⓒ c ⓓ b

Page 6

1.
   a. i N ii My parents want – I hate the idea – spend a week on a boat
   b. i N ii We are going to leave our suitcases – while we eat in the bar
   c. i N ii I would like – with tourist information about the city – please
   d. i N ii My father – always drove – because – my mother didn't have her
   e. i V ii When you leave the station – you have to – right – cross the road

2.
   a. crucero: cruise, consigna: left-luggage office, folleto: leaflet
   b. permiso: licence, torcer: turn

3.
   a. My parents want to do a cruise but I hate the idea of spending a week on a boat.
   b. We are going to leave our suitcases in the left-luggage office while we eat in the bar.
   c. I would like a brochure with tourist information about the city, please.
   d. My father always drove because my mother didn't have her licence.
   e. When you leave the station, you have to turn right and cross the road.

Page 7

Exam-style question

1 B   2 A   3 A   4 C

Page 8

Exam-style question

1 A   2 C   3 A   4 B   5 C

Page 9

Exam-style question from Page 3

1 D   2 E   3 G   4 F   5 A

Unit 2

Page 11

1.
   1 How do the most studious students feel about exams?
   2 What is the best way to reduce anxiety when facing exams?
   3 What is the main recommendation for revision?
   4 What should a good revision plan allow time for?
   5 In addition to studying, what else must you do during the revision period?

Page 12

1. (circled) estudiante, recreo, clases, asistir, intimidación, alumno, deportes, participar
2. (ticked) In Spanish, Full sentence, Lifted from the text, Short statement
3.
   1 wrong language
   2 too short / information missing
   3 answer incomplete

Page 13

1. A d, B c, C a, D b
2. a, b and c (see table below)

Question	Sentence identified in text	Does the information in the sentence answer the question?
2 ¿Cuántos estudiantes asisten al instituto?	'Asisten más de mil estudiantes y está situado en un barrio residencial de la pequeña ciudad.'	Yes: but it gives information about where the school is as well, which would not be relevant. Make sure you include the más de as well as mil as it is part of the answer.
3 ¿Por qué Alejandro piensa que son elegantes? Da dos razones.	'Todos los alumnos tienen un aspecto elegante porque llevan un uniforme azul.'	No: only one of the reasons is in the 'elegant' sentence; the other reason is in the following sentence: Además, tienen los zapatos bien limpios.
4 ¿Qué llevan los alumnos en el instituto de Alejandro?	'Todos los alumnos tienen un aspecto elegante porque llevan un uniforme azul.'	No: this refers to what the English students wear. He talks about the Mexican students in a later sentence: los estudiantes mexicanos con sus vaqueros y zapatillas de deporte.
5 ¿Qué aspecto del horario no le gusta a Alejandro?	'Quizás la diferencia más notable es el horario.'	No: this just points out that he finds the timetable different. The following sentence tells us that he feels sorry for students who only finish at 3.30 p.m.: ¡Los pobres no terminan hasta las tres y media!
6 ¿Qué le gustaría ver en su propio instituto?	'Es un aspecto que tenemos que mejorar en mi propio instituto en México.'	No: he doesn't say which aspect he is referring to. The information is in the previous sentence and divided into two parts, both of which are needed: después de las clases, ofrecen una gran cantidad de actividades y deportes.

Page 14

1

	Text	Question
b	Después del inglés ~~y la química, la informática suele ser la tercera asignatura más popular~~, según una encuesta reciente.	What is the most popular subject these days?
	Explanation: Chemistry and IT come after English, so English is the most popular subject.	
c	Cuando hace buen tiempo, suelo ir al instituto en bicicleta ~~pero durante el invierno mi madre me lleva en el coche. Nunca voy a pie.~~	How does this student get to school in summer?
	Explanation: The travel by car happens in the winter, the student never walks to school and the 'hace buen tiempo' makes the link between good weather and summer.	
d	~~Dejé mis deberes de historia porque no entendí la tarea~~ y acabo de terminar los ejercicios de matemáticas. ~~Estoy a punto de hacer el ensayo para religión.~~	Which homework has this student completed?
	Explanation: 'acabo de terminar' means 'I have just finished' whereas 'dejé' means 'I left' and 'estoy a punto de hacer' means 'I am about to do', so the student has completed their maths homework.	

Page 15

Exam-style question

1 the attention of adults

2 listening to others

3 persevering with a task until we complete it

4 subjects

5 the requirements for work and life in general

Page 16

Exam-style question

1 ansiedad

2 un euro cincuenta

3 ropa y accesorios de marca

4 hace tres semanas

5 perder la amistad de Carlos

6 ha encontrado a otros compañeros

Page 17

Exam-style question from Page 10

1 education is compulsory up to the age of 16

2 the wide range of subjects that they offer

3 students get individual attention (from the teachers)

4 in the list of exam results

Exam-style question from Page 11

1 stressed / they find them stressful

2 prepare well and in good time

3 it has to be active

4 all subjects and rest

5 relax and sleep well

Unit 3

Page 18

1 **a**

2 Me encantaría oírle recitar un capítulo de este libro.

3 Voy a dar la bienvenida a los jugadores que triunfaron en el torneo.

4 ¡Qué ilusión! Puedo conocer a mi actriz favorita de la tele.

5 Me encantaría ver una actuación en directo de un programa bien conocido.

b

A	La estrella de la pequeña pantalla, Marta López, estará en la librería Santos el sábado 15 de julio para lanzar su nuevo libro, sobre su vida y experiencias.
C	Los aficionados de la Copa Mundial disfrutarán del regreso de la selección nacional a la capital el sábado y de su vuelta de la ciudad en un autobús abierto.
D	Si quieres ver a tus actores y actrices favoritos en vivo, hay entradas para la grabación de la telenovela popular *La calle paralelo* este mes.
F	El autor célebre, Juan del Pozo, leerá extractos de su última novela *Naufragio* durante la Fiesta de la Lectura a principios de agosto.

Page 20

1 **a** **i** (underlined – question) club, Iván

(underlined – text) sí tengo ganas de aprender el ajedrez

ii (crossed out – text) Carlos piensa asistir, Perdí interés en los videojuegos de niño, Quizás optaría por el debate si pudiera entender los eventos actuales en el mundo.

iii (answer) chess club (justification: fancies learning chess; lost interest in video games when a child; doesn't understand world events enough to join debating club)

b **i** (underlined – question) Laura prefer

(underlined – text) ahora me he acostumbrado a usar una tableta, me parece más cómoda, Suelo confundirme con la trama cuando escucho los audiolibros

ii (crossed out – text) Antes insistía en leer los libros tradicionales

iii (answer) tablet (justification: she's got used to it / it's more comfortable; used to read books in the past; gets confused about the plot when listening to audiobooks)

c i (underlined – question) Gustavo, play

    (underlined – text) Desde el año pasado, me entusiasmo por el baloncesto.

  ii (crossed out – text) En la escuela primaria era fanático del fútbol, en la secundaria descubrí lo divertido que era el voleibol

  iii (answer) basketball (justification: he has been keen on it for a year; was keen on football in primary school; volleyball was fun in secondary school)

Page 21

①

Spanish	English
mentir	to lie
significar	to mean
evitar	to avoid
prohibido	forbidden
tener razón	to be right
cierto	true
equivocarse	to be mistaken

②

	Statement	Summary		Reason
a	<u>Nada me pareció más hermosa</u> que mi primera vista del mar a los siete años.	It was the best view I had seen.	✓	It means 'nothing was more beautiful than my first view of the sea…'
b	<u>Nadie tenía la menor idea</u> de cuánto echaba de menos a familia esos primeros días.	I didn't really miss my family at first.		It means 'no one had the slightest idea how much I missed my family…'
c	Solían decir <u>que los niños no se interesaban en leer</u>. Con los libros sobre el chico mágico, <u>esto ya no es el caso</u>.	Children aren't interested in reading any more.		It means 'children didn't used to read… this is no longer the case'
d	Imagina mi vergüenza cuando descubrí que <u>no había mandado el mensaje a Pablo sino a mi Papá</u>.	She had sent the wrong message to her boyfriend.		It means 'I hadn't sent the message to Pablo but to my Dad'.

Page 23

Exam-style question

1 A, E

2 1 unwinding / switching off at the end of the day

    2 losing herself in the story

Page 24

Exam-style question

1 C   2 C   3 B   4 A

Exam-style question from Page 19

1 B   2 F   3 C   4 A   5 D

---

② a i no significa que

      ii He can't afford to go out.

  b i se equivocó cuando

     ii half past eight

  c i no tienes razón

     ii Sevilla

  d i evitamos

     ii stay at home

  e i no es cierto

     ii keyboard

  f i estaba prohibido

     ii had a sandwich on the beach

Page 22

① a nadie: no one / nobody

  b ninguno: none / not … any

  c nada: nothing / not … anything

  d sino: but

  e jamás: never / ever

  f ya no: no longer / not any more

Unit 4

Page 26

①

Adjective / Noun	Verb form in the text	Infinitive form	Meaning
aburrido	aburren	aburrir	to bore
alegre	alegra	alegrar	to cheer up
decepcionante	decepcionó	decepcionar	to disappoint
entretenido	entretener	entretener	to entertain
helado/hielo	heló	helar	to freeze

Page 28

1 i and ii (noun underlined)

- **a** dar <u>apoyo</u> = apoyar – to support
- **b** servir como <u>guía</u> = guiar – to guide
- **c** hacer una <u>pregunta</u> = preguntar – to ask
- **d** dar una <u>explicación</u> = explicar – to explain
- **e** hacer un <u>dibujo</u> = dibujar – to draw
- **f** hacer una <u>grabación</u> = grabar – to record
- **g** dar <u>empleo</u> = emplear – to employ
- **h** tener un <u>fracaso</u> = fracasar – to fail
- **i** hacer un <u>diseño</u> = diseñar – to design
- **j** ser <u>molesto</u> = molestar – to disturb/annoy

2 (circled)

- **a** stopped
- **b** stolen
- **c** solved
- **d** delayed
- **e** fill in
- **f** contains
- **g** tired
- **h** complained

Page 29

1
- **a** lavar – to wash, levantarse – to get up, llegar – to arrive, llevar – to take / carry / wear, pedir – to ask for, perder – to lose, poder – to be able
- **b**
  - i   levanto
  - ii perdió
  - iii llegaron
  - iv puedes
  - v   llevaba
  - vi pedir
  - vii lavando
  - viii perdido

2 **a** and **b**

A	B	Meaning
comenzar	empezar	to start, begin
andar	caminar	to walk
tirar	echar	to throw
pasar	ocurrir	to happen
querer	desear	to want, desire
molestar	fastidiar	to bother, annoy
mandar	enviar	to send
mostrar	enseñar	to show

Page 30

1
- **a** to be worth (it)
- **b** to start to
- **c** to feel like
- **d** to stop ...ing
- **e** to have just…
- **f** to tend to
- **g** to continue to…

2 **a** A **b** B **c** C **d** A **e** C **f** C **g** A

Page 31

Exam-style question

1 His father thought it would be good for his discipline.

2 He didn't want to take part and complained every week.

3 He was guided and supported by his teachers / the guidance and support of his teachers

4 He missed his family and it bothered him being separated from his wife and daughter.

5 He has designed choreography for several productions.

Page 32

Exam-style question

1 No: he is up by 8am.

2 Yes: he will really miss the local library that is closing.

3 Yes: if he discovers he has been playing a videogame for two hours he will stop playing immediately.

Page 33

Exam-style question from Page 27

1 There was an icy wind / It was freezing in the wind / very cold and windy.

2 He was disappointed by the lack of goals.

3 1 The atmosphere in the stadium cheers him up.
  2 He enjoys being in the company of his friends.

4 He was surprised to find out it is so popular.

5 They assured him it is a fascinating activity.

Unit 5

Page 35

1
- **a** (circled) Hace un año, De momento, el abril que viene
- **b** (underlined) pasó, estuvo, fui, está visitando, se divierte, se encontrarán

2
- **a** I will park the car here.
- **b** We are going to buy return tickets.
- **c** Are you going to go by boat?
- **d** We will leave the cases at the left luggage office.
- **e** I'm going to complain about the noise.
- **f** The train is soon going to stop at the station.
- **g** You will enjoy yourselves in Malaga.
- **h** The children will return/go back to the (swimming) pool this afternoon.

3
- **a** (underlined) iban, salían, pasamos, estuve, fue, disfrutó, pensó, era, viajaban, podían, gustaban, teníamos, resolvimos, decidimos
- **b** and **c**

Preterite	English translation	Imperfect	English translation
pasamos (1pp)	we spent	iban (3pp)	they went / used to go
estuve (1ps)	I was	salían (3pp)	they turned out
fue (3ps)	it was	era (3ps)	it was
disfrutó (3ps)	he enjoyed	viajaban (3pp)	they travelled / used to travel
pensó (3ps)	he thought	podían (3pp)	they could
resolvimos (1pp)	we solved	gustaban (3pp)	they liked
decidimos (1pp)	we decided	teníamos (1pp)	they had / used to have

Page 36

1 (highlighted: near future, future)

a El sábado fuimos a la playa pero el lunes vamos a pasar el día en el parque acuático.

b En mayo habrá una fiesta porque es el día del santo patrón del pueblo.

c Compré este recuerdo pero voy a devolverlo porque está roto.

d Tuvimos mucha suerte con el tiempo pero creo que lloverá pronto.

e Voy a mirar los detalles ahora y reservaré el hotel mañana.

2 **a** I only visited México once.

b Every year we used to eat in the same restaurant.

c We used to spend the mornings on the beach.

d My parents hired a car.

e When I was skiing in Italy, I broke my leg.

3 (circled) present; (underlined) near future; (highlighted) future, preterite, imperfect

Prefiero ir al extranjero cuando voy de vacaciones porque en general hace más calor. De pequeño, no prestaba mucha atención al tiempo porque siempre lo pasaba bien jugando en la playa. Recuerdo un día cuando mis padres tuvieron que arrastrarme de la playa porque había una tormenta enorme. Ahora el sol me importa más y sobre todo la semana próxima porque vamos a estar en Lanzarote. El pronóstico dice que hará buen tiempo aparte de miércoles cuando va a haber viento.

4 **a** ¿Por qué Paula prefiere ir al extranjero de vacaciones?

b Cuando Paula era pequeña, ¿cómo reaccionaba al tiempo?

c ¿Qué hicieron sus padres el día de la gran tormenta?

d ¿Qué van a hacer la semana que viene?

e ¿Por qué no van a ir a la playa el miércoles?

Page 37

1 **a** and **b**

Spanish	English	P/N/F
de momento	at the moment	N
pasado mañana	the day after tomorrow	F
anteayer	the day before yesterday	P
dentro de tres días	in three days	F
hace una semana	a week ago	P
esta noche	tonight	F
anoche	last night	P
en el porvenir	in the future	F

2 **a**, **b** and **c**

Time phrase	Refers to verb	Verb tense
Hace un siglo	era	imperfect
en esos días	tenía	imperfect
durante los años setenta	Se convirtió	preterite
En este momento	está tratando	present continuous
en los meses que vienen	hay	present
La semana próxima	se abrirá	future

3 **i** and **ii**

a puedo (present) – De momento

b decidimos (preterite) – Anoche

c voy a empezar (near future) – A partir de mañana

d estaré (future) – El sábado que viene

e ganaron (preterite) – hace tres meses

Page 38

1 **a** A mi abuela le gustan los recuerdos y le compré un abanico en la tienda.
  i *compré*: I – 1st person singular
  ii subject: I
  iii object pronoun: le = her / the grandmother
  iv translation: My grandmother likes souvenirs and I bought her a fan in the shop.

b Tu novia te manda un mensaje todos los días, ¿verdad?
  i *manda*: he/she/ it – 3rd person singular
  ii subject: girlfriend
  iii object pronoun: te = you
  iv translation: Your girlfriend sends you a message every day, doesn't she?

c Los niños hacían mucho ruido y una señora anciana les gritó.
  i *gritó*: he / she / it – 3rd person singular
  ii subject: elderly lady
  iii object pronoun: les = them / the children
  iv translation: The children were making a lot of noise and an elderly lady shouted at them.

2 **a** I found them on the floor. – Las encontré en el suelo.

b He explained the problem to us. – Nos explicó el problema.

c I'll send you the photos. – Te mandaré las fotos.

Page 39

1 **a** (imperfect) sentíamos, teníamos, íbamos, queríamos, estaba, daban, estaba, decía

(preterite) cambió, Fuimos

(future) tendrán

(near future) van a encontrarnos, va a dar

(time phrases) durante todo el año, esta mañana, en seguida, de momento, mañana por la tarde

b (imperfect) sentían(1), había(2)

(preterite) estaban(2), fueron(4)

(future) tendrán(6)

(near future) van a pasar(5)

(time phrases) antes de(1), esta noche(5)

(2) The receptionist is treating us very well and the company is going to give me compensation.

Exam-style question

1 muy emocionados

2 todo estaba sucio y las ventanas daban a un aparcamiento

3 estaba mucho más lejos de la playa de lo que decía en el sitio web

4 a la recepción

5 en un hotel

6 mañana por la tarde

Page 40

Exam-style question

1 F   2 N   3 P   4 P   5 F

Page 41

Exam-style question from Page 34

1 P   2 P   3 N   4 F   5 N

Unit 6

Page 42

(1) **a** Jogging (underlined): Es refrescante correr en el parque. / Cuando voy por la ciudad el aire no es puro.

Reading (circled): Leo sobre todo novelas de fantasía. / Encuentro la lectura muy relajante.

Mobile phones (highlighted): Mi hijo Leo es adicto a su móvil. / Malgasta tanto tiempo mirando la pantalla.

b Jogging = P+N

Reading = P

Mobile phones = N

Page 44

(1) (positive adjectives) afortunado, precioso, cortés, genial, educado, atento

(negative adjectives) cobarde, torpe, decepcionante, antipático, asqueroso, avaro, nocivo, inseguro, celoso, vago

(2) **a** and **b**

Spanish	P/N	English
tener suerte	P	to be lucky
disfrutar	P	to enjoy
Enfadar	N	to anger
estar harto de	N	to be fed up with
fastidiar	N	to annoy
tener miedo	N	to be afraid
sonreírse	P	to smile
tener ganas	P	to feel like (doing something)

(3) add yellow highlight to 'positive' and blue highlight to 'negative':]

(highlighted: positive, negative)

a antipática, fastidió, N

b vago, sonreír, P+N

c cortés, atento, desconsiderado, P+N

d Vale la pena, preciosos, P

e No hemos tenido mucha suerte, estoy harto de, N

f geniales, me decepcionó, P + N

g Me enfada, excesivos, N

h Disfruté, tengo ganas de, P

Page 45

(1)

	Description	Emoji
a	Esta fue la oportunidad que siempre había buscado, fue un sueño convertido en realidad. Tenía ganas de cantar, de correr y de besar a todo el mundo.	happy / delighted
b	Esta fue su primera actuación en público. Patricia tenía la boca seca y las manos temblaban; estaba segura que olvidaría la música o se caería antes de llegar al piano.	nervous
c	Susana salió del salón, cerrando la puerta ruidosamente. Sus padres eran tan antipáticos, prohibiéndola que fuera al concierto con su novio. Quería gritar.	angry
d	Al leer el mensaje, Elisa estuvo a punto de llorar. Había imaginado un futuro junto con Carlos y ahora, con estas pocas palabras, su futuro entero había desaparecido.	sad

(2) (a) No entiendo la atracción de esa fiesta. ¿Por qué malgastar toda esa comida y cubrirte de tomates para limpiar todo una hora después?
(N) She thinks it's pointless.

(b) Esta no es una fiesta a punto de desaparecer. Los hoteles están llenos y cada año vienen más visitantes, de aquí y del resto del mundo.
(P) He thinks it's more and more popular.

(c) ¿Una merienda en la playa? No sé si has visto el pronóstico pero dicen que habrá viento en la costa con riesgo de chubascos.
(N) He thinks the weather will be bad.

Page 46

(1) Yes: She gets up early because she has things to do.

(2) The quiz question and the circled answer, but not the other two quiz answers.

(3) First incorrect answer: This answer ignores the question where we learn that Elena gets up early to get things done.

Second incorrect answer: This answer leaves out half the circled answer where Elena says she has things to do.

(4) (a) They have not read the quiz question and used it in the answer.

(b) No: She does her homework on the bus on the way to school.

Page 47

(1) (a) (underlined)

weather: hizo un frío intolerable y un viento helado soplaba

bonfire: La hoguera era enorme e impresionante y también, afortunadamente, daba bastante calor – lo que apreciábamos.

food: comida caliente: hamburguesas, perros calientes y patatas asadas en el horno. Probé un perro caliente y lo encontré asqueroso, de muy baja calidad. Sin embargo, la hamburguesa era riquísima y devoré cada bocado

fireworks: el espectáculo de fuegos artificiales. La primera parte fue lenta, incluso aburrida; y me sentí decepcionada, pero al poco rato mejoró muchísimo y hubo luces y colores por todas partes del cielo.

(b) (highlighted) intolerable; helado; enorme; impresionante; afortunadamente; calor (in the context of the text); apreciábamos; asqueroso; baja calidad; riquísima; La primera parte fue lenta, incluso aburrida, y me sentí decepcionada; mejoró muchísimo

(c) (circled) y; también; Sin embargo; pero

Exam-style question

1 N   2 P   3 P+N   4 P+N

Page 48

(1) (a) (underlined)

Question 1: atraídos por una nueva experiencia y por el reto de enfrentarse al miedo que dan estos deportes

Question 2: Hace menos de un mes murió un joven practicando el parapente en las playas de Benidorm. En doce meses ha habido cuatro accidentes mortales de jóvenes que practicaban este deporte en la zona.

Question 3: los accidentes se producen por negligencias de jóvenes que no toman en serio el peligro

Question 4: "No estamos satisfechos con la situación y estamos intentando regular más estos deportes. Además, queremos cambiar la ley para que no puedan comprar material de vuelo sin el permiso de la Federación."

(b) (highlighted) nueva, reto, miedo, murió, accidentes mortales, negligencias, el peligro, No estamos satisfechos

(c) (circled) Además

Exam-style question

1 B

2 C

3 careless young people who don't take the danger seriously

4 No: they want to regulate the sport more / they want to change the law.

Page 49

Exam-style question from Page 42

1 N   2 P   3 P   4 P+N

Exam-style question from Page 43

1 A   2 C   3 B   4 C

Unit 7

Page 50

(1) (a) accountant
(b) lawyer
(c) postman
(d) farmer

Page 52

(1) Student's own answers.

(2) i, ii

(a) ¿Qué trabajo quería hacer José?

What job did José want to do?

(b) Cómo sabemos que Sara se había organizado bien para la entrevista?

How do we know Sara was well organised for the interview?

(c) ¿Cuál fue la conclusión de Carlos al final de su primer día?

What was Carlos's conclusion at the end of his first day?

(d) ¿Cuándo empieza Laura su nuevo trabajo como profesora?

When does Laura start her new job as a teacher?

(3) (underlined)

- **a** ser el jefe de una oficina entera
- **b** estaba bien vestida, bien preparada y puntual
- **c** aceptar el trabajo había sido un gran error
- **d** empieces el mes que viene

(4) **a** jefe de una oficina (entera)

- **b** estaba bien vestida, bien preparada y puntual
- **c** aceptar el trabajo había sido un gran error
- **d** el mes que viene

Page 53

(1) **a** , **b** and **c**

Spanish	Looks like	Really means	Memorable phrase
sano	sane	healthy	un sapo sano (a healthy toad)
campo	camp	field, countryside	camping en el campo (camping in the country)
lectura	lecture	reading	la lectura perdura (Reading lasts)
sensible	sensible	sensitive	el combustible es sensible (the fuel is sensitive)
éxito	exit	success	un éxito médico (a medical success)
arena	arena	sand	arena chilena (Chilean sand)
actual	actual	current	la cathedral actual (the current cathedral)

(2) **a** The ~~number~~ of the company is Coltran. – name

- **b** I'm going to the ~~library~~ to buy a novel. – bookshop
- **c** The taxi ~~conductor~~ caused the accident. – driver
- **d** The ~~carpet~~ contains my university notes. – file
- **e** How funny! It's a very ~~gracious~~ joke. – funny, amusing

(3) **a** and **b**

Spanish word in text (underlined)	False friend meaning	Real meaning
decepción	deception	disappointment
sucedía (suceder)	to succeed	to happen
soportaba (soportar)	to support	to bear, stand
últimamente	ultimately	lately, recently
asistirás (asisitir a)	to assist	to attend
realizarás (realizar)	to realise	to undertake, carry out
formación	formation	training
recordar	to record	remember

Page 54

(1) **a** empaquetaron:

- i preterite
- ii they
- iii parcel
- iv me

b Noruega:

- i the name of a person or place
- ii 'at' or 'to'
- iii Norway

c They parcelled me off to Norway

(2) experto – expert, sagas – saga, poemas – poems, épicos – epic, nórdicos – Nordic, batallas – battles

(3) **a** adjective of nationality

- **b** Icelandic

(4) **a** send him to Norway (to stay) with a family he didn't know

- **b** an Icelandic king from the sagas
- **c** epic poems full of blood, battles and chopped-off heads
- **d** she worked in a chocolate factory

Page 55

Exam-style question

1 organising / tidying the store in the back of the shop and looking after regular customers

2 No: he didn't put his head or his heart into it.

3 It was getting lively / They needed an additional member of staff.

4 half detective, half poet

5 someone who would be cheap (to employ) and who wasn't afraid of impossible missions

Page 56

Exam-style question

1 B   2 A   3 A   4 C

Page 57

Exam-style question from Page 51

1 a crime novel and a romantic poem

2 an instruction manual for a washing machine

3 translating film subtitles

4 a broad vocabulary and love of precision

5 Translators must look after their posture and eyesight as they spend many hours in front of a computer.

Unit 8

Page 59

1 con – with, en – in/on, por – for/through/by, de – of/from, entre – between/among, sin – without, desde – from/since, para – in order to/for, sobre – on/about

Page 60

1
a all

b more than

c any more

d almost / nearly

2 (missing words underlined)

a There is a lot of traffic and <u>therefore</u> the pollution is harmful.

b This animal is <u>another</u> species in danger of extinction.

c The oil tanker sank at <u>about</u> three in the morning.

d There is <u>still</u> a lot to be done in order to protect the rainforest.

3
a This law will not solve the problem of packaging either.

b Drug addiction is even worse among the homeless.

c The greenhouse effect is perhaps the most urgent topic.

d We have already seen several accidents this year.

e I am quite worried about the lack of equality at work.

Page 61

1
a To have a job at the swimming pool I need a (first-aid) certificate.

b The good thing is that they say there are fewer (holes) in the ozone layer.

c In some countries the (waste) from the factories still goes into / enters the rivers.

2
a Translation: After the fuel leak from the petrol tanker, the <u>oil spill</u> is affecting the animals and birds on the coast.

Notes: *negra* means black, *marea* contains *mar* = sea; the words fuel / leak / tanker / affecting animals and birds – context implies some sort of pollution

b Translation: We want to take <u>blankets</u> to the homeless: they will be better than the old newspapers that they use.

Notes: context implies *mantas* are something that would replace the newspapers that homeless people use to wrap themselves in

c Translation: With the lack of exercise and all the fast food restaurants, <u>obesity</u> is a serious problem in our society.

Notes: *sobrepeso* – *sobre* = over/above; *peso* = weight; context is about a problem arising from lack of exercise and poor diet

d Translation: Without significant rain in two years, the country is suffering the worst <u>drought</u> in 50 years.

Notes: *sequía* – word family: *seco* = dry, *secar* = to dry; context refers to the result of no rain for two years; preceded by 'the worst' so a noun is required

3 (translation) Yesterday we had a class on / about the dangers of smoking. The teacher explained the medical effects very simply so that it was easy to understand. Furthermore, he warned us of the other disadvantages like the revolting smell and the yellowish colour of the teeth. I left the class completely convinced that I was never going to smoke in my life.

(translation notes)

tabaquismo – word family: *tabaco* = tobacco; contextual clues including *fumar* on last line

sencillamente – grammar clue: *-mente* = -ly so an adverb; following phrase 'so it was easy to understand' helps narrow down the meaning

advirtió – context says 'he ...ed us about the other disadvantages', so must be verb of communicating

asqueroso – word family: *asco / qué asco* – disgust; context tells us it's an adjective describing the smell of smoke

amarillento – word family: *amarillo* = yellow; context – the colour of teeth through smoking

convencida – similar to the English 'convinced', past participle *-ido* has 'ed' as equivalent

jamás – French students may note similarity to *jamais*; context of being absolutely convinced about not smoking may suggest an emphatic negative is needed

Page 62

1 por todas partes – everywhere; esta noche – tonight; quedar en – to agree to; pasarlo bien – to have a good time

2
a <u>spent it very well</u> – had a very/really good time

b <u>in all parts</u> – everywhere

c <u>stayed in</u> – agreed to

d <u>this night</u> – tonight

3
a ~~The~~ drug addiction is a serious problem in ~~the~~ society.

b ~~The~~ women suffer ~~the~~ discrimination in the world of work.

c In the next fifty years we have to solve the problem of ~~the~~ global warming.

4
a On the one hand, the temperatures are less extreme but, on the other (hand), floods are more frequent.

b I am seventeen (years old). My birthday was two weeks ago.

c I don't understand that word. What does it mean?

d She is a geography teacher in my sister's school.

Page 63

Exam-style question

Sample translation:

Every year our school organises a week of charity activities and the students undertake voluntary work. Last October I helped in a home for the elderly and I played the piano in the residents' lounge. Next week I will be in the city preparing hot soup for the homeless.

Page 64

Exam-style question

Sample translation:

Last night we had a storm in the village / town with heavy rain for three hours. This morning floods continue to affect the centre and many houses are under water. There is rubbish everywhere and my friends and I have agreed to take part in the clean-up operation. Global warming has unexpected effects!

Page 65

Exam-style question from Page 58

Sample translation:

In spite of the bad weather, Ana is on the beach, helping to remove the rubbish from the sea and the sand. "We have seen a programme about the effects of plastic on the fish and animals of the ocean. These bags and bottles will harm the marine life and we are going to clean up this part of the coast."

Exam question from Page 59

Sample translation:

Are you overweight? Do you want to lose a few pounds/ kilos? It's much easier to achieve this aim/goal if you become a member of a club. Here we offer advice and ideas for meals that are delicious but low in calories. With our support you will have a slim and healthy body. "I went to the club and I lost eleven kilos in three weeks", says Luisa.

Unit 9

Page 66

1   She used her knowledge of their personality and skills to help them with problems in science.

2   They felt ashamed because they knew they had disappointed her.

3   They behaved like stupid, naughty children in her class.

4   She must have hated them.

Page 67

1 C   2 A   3 A   4 B

Page 68

1   B, D

2   (any two of:)

leave the family home / search for her real father / face her father with the truth that she was his daughter

Page 69

1   (any two of:)

es muy saludable / les ayudará a hacer más amigos / aporta ventajas que siguen teniendo impacto durante toda la vida

2   porque conocen (como nadie) el carácter y las habilidades de sus hijos

3   el equipo y el transporte

4   deben ponerse a practicar algún deporte

Page 70

1 A   2 B   3 C   4 B

Page 71

1   a (real) work of art

2   No: he says you can get it removed if you change your mind later on / later in life.

3   She thinks they are / look dirty and are too permanent.

4   They can cause skin infections and you might get a disease like AIDS.

Page 72

1   C, E

2   1 They take place at the local / nearest university.

2 They last (about) three days.

Page 73

Exam-style question A

1 C   2 F   3 B   4 E   5 A

Exam-style question B

Sample translation:

My older brother Santi has an interview on Thursday and he is very nervous. There is a lot of unemployment in the city and there are few well paid jobs. Santi is going to research the company so that he can ask the boss intelligent questions. He has already bought a new suit and planned the journey.

LRC
WITHDRAWN GE
SWINDON

Notes